SHIFTING SHADOWS

OF

SUPERNATURAL POWER

SHIFTING SHADOWS

OF

SUPERNATURAL POWER

JULIA C. LOREN

WITH MAHESH CHAVDA AND BILL JOHNSON

DESTINY IMAGE® PUBLISHERS, INC.
P.O. Box 310, Shippensburg, PA 17257-0310

*"Speaking to the Purposes of God for this
Generation and for the Generations to Come."*

This book and all other Destiny Image, Revival Press, Mercy Place, Fresh Bread, Destiny Image Fiction, and Treasure House books are available at Christian bookstores and distributors worldwide.

For a U.S. bookstore nearest you, call 1-800-722-6774.
For more information on foreign distributors, call 717-532-3040.
Or reach us on the Internet: **www.destinyimage.com**

ISBN 10: 0-7684-2369-4
ISBN 13: 978-0-7684-2369-3

For Worldwide Distribution, Printed in the U.S.A.
7 8 9 10 11 / 16 15 14 13 12

Acknowledgements

To those who contributed to this manuscript by writing excerpts specifically for use in this book or by granting interviews...Thank you for giving your time. To everyone I quoted, thank you for mentoring us through your ministries and nudging us into greater levels of faith and understanding.

To my dear friends who survived the writing of this book—Steve and Michele Saunders...Thank you for housing me for weeks on end when I needed a place to write, praying for me while I wrote, having just the right books on your shelves, and extending so much grace and love to me in the course of our friendship over the last 15 years.

To Graham, Bill, and Mahesh...Thank you for being so openhearted and openhanded. You are true examples of ones who not only persevere in ministry at great personal sacrifice, but ones who burn ever brighter—continuing to illuminate our path and chase the shifting shadows of darkness from our lives and from many cultures.

To Abba...Thank you for standing over my shoulder as I wrote and offering suggestions.

Endorsements

I have known Julia Loren for 20 plus years as pastor, friend, and fellow pilgrim. I've watched her grow in wisdom, understanding, and that most useful of spiritual gifts—discernment. What she writes is always worth reading. She will frustrate some because she asks too many questions and provides too few answers. I guess that's the journalist in her. But she will make you think. She is one of those Jesus-followers who is not in lockstep with the latest fad, but who is willing to listen for the voice of the Master and help tune others' ears to hear Him.

Ed Cook, Senior Pastor
Vineyard Christian Fellowship of Seattle
Seattle, Washington

In today's spiritual climate, vast shades of gray seem to overpower the well defined boundaries previously called black and white. The need of the hour is for discernment. True discernment restores boundaries, dispels fear, and creates a safe environment where authentic spiritual experiences can flourish. Julia Loren comes to our aid in her must-read book *Shifting*

Shadows of Spiritual Power by re-establishing proper guidelines for those in spiritual quest.

James W. Goll

Cofounder of Encounters Network

Author of *The Seer, Dream Language* and *The Lost Art of Intercession*

Table of Contents

PART THREE

Foreword

Real prophets are challenged by mediocrity. They have an inner compulsion to fight darkness. They become light. Mediocrity is the shadow land of faith to them. In the original showdown between God and the prophets of Baal, Elijah was not just fighting with occult powers. He was challenging the space between dark and light; the grey areas; the shifting shadows of loyalty which people can inhabit when they do not reside in the light, close to the beacon of faithfulness.

Prophets live in the light, walk in the light, and bask in the light of all that God is to His people. They live with upturned faces to a God who perpetually lifts up the light of His countenance over His people. God smiles, and we look to Him, and our faces are radiant.

We have a cell in our DNA that loves to worship, we exist to magnify. If not God, it will be something or someone else, an idol of some sort.

Real prophets adore intimacy with God. They love His presence. It is their place of refuge, a fortress, a secret place of worship and communion. They access a place of blinding, coruscating light. From that place they embark on their mission to magnify the Lord in the world of men. The chief role of a prophet is to make God radiant to everyone they meet, be it friend or foe; Christian or pre-Christian; the good and the wicked.

Prophets live in the center of light, not on the edge of darkness. Their influence and anointing stretches out to touch the blackness and invade it, but they themselves have their heart safely locked away in the inviolate place of God's affection. Everyone must come to the light and abide there. Too many Christians live in the shadows of intimacy and are therefore not overwhelmed by God. They are in control of their passion instead of being abandoned to it.

Intimacy provokes confidence which releases faith to stand in God's presence and see Him as big as he is. Prophets declare the hugeness of God in all His attributes. God is looking for a people who will make Him bigger.

Our intimacy with God intimidates the enemy. It will also offend Christians living in a controlled, passionless relationship with the Lord. Fundamentalists are usually no fun and mainly mental in their approach to God. The Father smiles, He laughs, He has a huge sense of humor. He laughs at His enemies.

Boldness comes from the heart of God. A confidence so rich it makes anything else seem like a poverty spirit. Elijah had fun on Mount Carmel. Prophets relish the battle. Elijah ridiculed the enemy.

The Church at large has too much respect for the devil and not enough admiration for the Lord. When we live in the radiance of God our hearts are captivated by His brilliance. Our focus is sharp, our perceptions in high definition. We are captured by the immensity of the Father. We live in shock and awe at what He can do, He really is far above all principalities and powers.

Shadow-land Christians seldom turn up for the fight. If they do, they look for a lead from someone else. Confidence takes the initiative. In shadow-land language, confidence is deemed to be triumphalism. If misery loves company, then mediocrity fellowships with doubt. "I believe, help my unbelief" is the cry of a man stumbling toward the light not away from it.

Elijah was not just attacking the darkness he was challenging the grey areas in the people round about him. We must see God's people walking in fullness, not measure. The enemy has come to steal, to kill, and destroy. A church living in less than what the Father has decreed is being robbed, their initiative killed, and their capacity to overcome destroyed. Mediocrity is what we are left with, if we do not live in the full light of His presence.

Prophets give a wake up call to the Body of Christ. Any sportsman will tell us that it is not possible to win if we are afraid to lose. Ironically it is Christians who live in the shadows who are most afraid of the dark.

If the power of the Cross condemns us to victory then we must produce believers who have a passionate desire to win. The showdown on Mount Carmel declared to God's people, "This is who God is! Who is He for you?"

New Testament prophets do not stand between God and man, only Jesus can do that. Rather they stand before God in the presence of man. They are not idealists. They are realists because they live in the presence of God in such a way that their reality is shaped by their intimacy.

The showdown was over before it began. Elijah was not fighting to get victory. He was contending from the place of overcoming: the presence of God. What God's people were witnessing was the power of God being expressed through the heart of a man who knew that His anointing came from his intimate relationship with the Lord.

Elijah couldn't lose—that's the significance of Mount Carmel.

Graham Cooke
Founder of Future Training Institute
Author and Church Consultant

Preface

The shifting shadows blurring the lines between light and darkness, good and evil, are creating a twilight zone of spiritual awareness, especially in North America. It results in confusion and apathy on one hand, or an inordinate desire for power at the other extreme. These shadows lead many to call evil "good" and good "evil" not only in society but within the walls of many churches. We must chase the shadows of confusion out of our minds.

Unless we purpose to dwell in the realms of God's glory—His love and light—we will easily be led astray into shifting shadows of loyalty and fail to reflect His magnificent radiance. He is the light that overcomes the darkness. In Him there is no shifting shadow, no shadow of turning. The intent of this book is to reveal the realms of God's glory and power increasing on the earth today. It is an increase that heralds the end of darkness, the end of the dark lord's power, and the beginning of the brilliant, majestic beauty of the second coming of Christ.

This book contains interviews and excerpts from many well-known prophetic voices who call people to step out of the shifting shadows of loyalties and into a passionate pursuit of the King of Kings and Lord of Lords, His glory, and the power inherent in His Kingdom. It is a call to take your place in the plan unfolding…a plan that heralds the close of this age.

By the end of the book, you will discover a measure of discernment about the origins of revelatory and supernatural spiritual power and the shadows of deception in the world and in the Church, to equip you to receive and express the fullness of the Kingdom of God. It is an unabashed attempt to move you into a greater measure of faith and power so you will stand in the fullness of awe, captivated by God's passionate love. Then, as bearers of light, the shadows will flee before you and the showdown of the clash of powers to come at the end of the age will give way to the eternal joys of His Kingdom come.

PART ONE

CHAPTER 1

The House of Shifting Shadows

Four children moved with their parents into a small house in a wealthy community near the sea. It seemed, at that stage in their lives, that the parents were mostly absent, either working or socializing, leaving the children to explore life on their own. There was nothing remarkable about the children. They were good looking, of average intelligence, fought one another as siblings do, played well with others, received good marks in citizenship in school, and they were active in sports. Prior to moving into their new home, they were two boys and two girls growing up together in a happy household. Once they moved into their new home, however, the happiness shifted and the fissures in the family cracked wide open. Too quickly, the resident shadows carried them, one by one, into great darkness.

Anyone who watches old horror movies knows that darkness often resides in the attic. Such hiding spaces attract children; so it was no surprise when Ann, the 13-year-old eldest daughter, crawled up into the small attic space above the hallway to see if the previous occupants had left anything behind. She saw only one object, a box heavy of old papers. She dragged the box to the edge of the attic steps and enlisted the help of Rick, her younger brother, to steady the ladder so she could bring the box down into the light for inspection. They opened it to find dozens of pamphlets and since the boy had no interest in reading he scampered off to surf with his friends as she sat down to read. Not knowing the meaning of many of the words, she pondered the term "Theosophical Society," then read a few pages about mysticism and spiritism and grew bored. She stuffed the box in her closet alongside her tennis racket.

Within a year great changes took place in every member of the household. The parents' stress doubled as they labored under a recessive economy resulting in job changes and financial duress beyond their ability to cope. So they did what many couples in Southern California do under stress—drink and ignore the growing cracks in their marriage. Karl, the eldest and natural born leader, grew very popular in his high school and was elected class president. He looked good, acted good, attracted girls, and could manipulate adults to obtain anything he wanted or wanted to do. In secret he experimented with a variety of drugs and gravitated toward an older group who engaged in reading secret books and performing secret rituals. Little brother Rick eventually followed his big brother's example.

Meanwhile, Ann pulled the Theosophical Society booklets out of the closet. Although she didn't understand them, she read them all and developed an appetite to experience something more transcendental than drugs could offer. She had little contact with her brothers who were gone most of the time and had scant interest in her sister, Tami, who was five years younger.

Although the house was small, none of the siblings had any idea what each other was into. The parents thought the children were happily busy in school, surfing, playing tennis, and other sports; and they approved of Karl's budding interest in the opposite sex and high grade point average. The children eventually realized that they all had discovered the world of marijuana in the same year and began to encourage each another to try mind-expanding drugs beyond weed.

The boys attended secret parties. Their personalities changed rapidly. Karl grew especially serious, withdrawn. Rumors at school about a satanist group led Ann to believe her brother was one of the key members. The dark rituals, orgies, the satanic bible, and talk about Anton LaVey, intrigued her but she decided she wasn't interested in that degree of evil. In the meanwhile, a Jesus People movement had arrived on campus and Ann gravitated toward a lighter brand of spirituality—to a God who offered love and healing. She could see that the dark side was clearly overtaking her brothers.

One day she came home from school to find Karl sound asleep on the couch speaking fluent German. Another time, she heard him talking to someone she couldn't see in the room with him, It was an entity that only he could see and later he told her was his "special friend." The rumors at school about a secret society and satanic sacrifices increased. Abruptly and unexpectedly, Karl graduated early and moved to Northern California. He drifted into an even darker morass of occultism associated with Anton LaVey.

Karl became entangled in a relationship with a woman who ardently practiced witchcraft, a woman Ann described as "radiating the presence of evil." Throughout the years she heard bits and pieces about her brother's lifestyle—rumors too evil to include in this book—things she hoped were not true. From time to time her brother brought strange friends home and what little he said about his life seemed to substantiate the rumors. When confronted, though, he became defensive and denied any involvement with the occult.

Karl's life continued to decline until he could barely carry on a conversation and often lapsed into brief flights of disconnected sentences, staring into space as if watching the sentences hang in the air like butterflies. He seemed completely possessed or completely mentally ill. In hindsight, his family came to see the signs of mental illness had, in fact, crept into Karl throughout his school years. Perhaps this predisposition to mental illness evolved because of the occult and drugs. Or, perhaps, the demonic preyed upon the young boy's mind and led him to be overtaken by the occult. Ann never could tell the difference.

Rick flowed in the occult for awhile, eventually deciding to make a living. He married and settled down to raise four children of his own. They live life as best they can.

Ann decided to give up reading Theosophy and her attraction to "white" magic and "prophets" like Edgar Cayce and Nostradamus. She stopped gardening for the local medium and shunned tarot card readings and invitations to spiritualist meetings. She gravitated instead toward the Christians and listened longingly to their talk about Jesus.

Not long after she graduated from high school, Ann left home to travel around the world. She eventually settled in Israel where she spent the better part of a year studying Hebrew and working on a kibbutz (a collective farming community) at the base of Mount Carmel near Haifa. One day, she walked through the community orchards at the base of the mountain with a fellow language student, a young Jewish woman, who pointed up the hillside and said, "Up there is where Elijah slew the prophets of Baal." Ann didn't know who Elijah was or who the prophets of Baal were, so the Jewish woman lent her a Bible to read. She told her it provided a history of the country and she showed her in which chapter she would find the story of Elijah.

The story about the prophets of Baal caught her attention. They cut themselves and danced madly because they were taunted by a prophet from God who challenged them to follow Him—the most powerful God. She noticed that there was a spiritual power that led to destruction and another spiritual power that led to the true God. As she read she considered her own experiences with spiritual power that were not of God and, though she would not understand it for many years, she sensed that Elijah's story was somehow entwined with her own. Over the next few weeks further Bible reading impacted her so much that one day she knelt on the floor of her room and asked Jesus to come into her heart and change her life.

Ann encountered Jesus in a remarkable way at Bethel Hostel in Haifa, a Christian mission that houses Charismatic church meetings. One Friday night, she received the baptism in the Holy Spirit—the presence of God filled her with the unconditional, overwhelming sense of love and joy that she had not even been aware of searching for.

During the weeks following her experience of the Holy Spirit, she realized that Heaven's revelatory realm had opened, enabling her to occasionally see angels and demons, receive words of knowledge about others' lives and

coming events, and dream prophetic dreams. After each encounter or experience she would return to her room, open her Bible and ask God, "Where's
that in Your book?" She soon discovered that the Bible was rich in stories
about spiritual encounters and power in both the Old and New Testaments.
The supernatural power she had once sought in herself or in the occult was
dark and oppressive. This power from God is something supernaturally-nat-
ural, full of joy, light, and peace. Now she knew the difference between dark
power and God's power.

Eventually, her letters home led her sister to accept Jesus. Her brothers
would also accept Christ, but they didn't shift out of the darkness and into the
light as she had. Perhaps it had something to do with the depths of their involvement with satanism and the entrapment of their wills. She may never know.

When she returned home to California, however, the richness of her encounter with God in Israel faded and she struggled greatly in her faith. The
emotional and spiritual battle raging within her caused her great distress and
she asked two elders in her church to set aside time to pray for her.

Not knowing the hold of darkness on her life and ignorant of the fact that
even those who believe in Jesus may need deliverance, they launched into
what they thought would be a short prayer session. As soon as they started
praying, Ann curled up into herself, her arms circling around her knees. She
started bouncing like a ball up against the shuttered doors of the choir robe
closet. They knew instantly that they were dealing with something demonic
and sent for the pastor. As they continued praying, she stopped bouncing and
seemed to fall into a trance.

Later, she described what she saw: A series of demonic images like scenes cut
from horror movies flashed before her eyes as if she were watching a movie
screen. Subtitles scrolled across the bottom of the screen. The words she read
were her own self-deprecating thoughts, temptations, traumatic events that impacted her, guilt and shame, and accusations against her—words she heard in
her head for years…words that originated with the father of lies, satan.

As they prayed, the images slowed down. The subtitles slowed as well.
Then, as each lie scrolled across the bottom of the screen projecting in her

mind, a Scripture flew out from the opposite direction and annihilated the lie. The Scriptures increased. The prayers increased. Finally, Ann felt what she described as a spirit, which had encased her entire being, lifting off of her. She sat quietly resting with her back against a wall, and then eventually sighed. It was over. What she thought must have been a 20 minute prayer session at most had lasted over two hours. She thought she had perhaps rested for a minute or two after the deliverance before opening her eyes. She had, in fact, rested in that place of peace for almost half an hour completely oblivious to others in the room.

In the following days, the light radiating from her face amazed everyone. There was no question about it. She was free. The undercurrent of mental chatter and temptation had been demolished and her mind was clear. In the weeks that followed she felt incredible joy.

Her sister Tami followed suit. She accepted Christ and attained a great measure of healing through both inner healing and counseling. Her early experiences developing her Christian faith and walk are now a distant memory. She is married, emotionally and financially stable, well-educated, and the mother of two beautiful children.

Two brothers and two sisters: Two chose the God who is light and love. Two bound themselves to the dark lord on his dark throne. Karl and Rick have not found total release from the oppressive spirits of the occult. Although they have backed away from overt evil, evil still controls their lives. They are shells of the men they could have become. Their minds, souls, and spirits are whispers of what they had once been. Now well into their 40s, their prognosis for recovery, even with extensive deliverance and psychotherapy, is not good. They have gone too far. Yet they may, one day, turn toward the Father of Light and receive a measure of joy and peace and love that they have never known and the quality of their lives will increase dramatically and eternally.

The shifting shadows of their childhood house by the sea brought all four of them into contact with great evil power and devious spiritual experiences. Had they only known that a little dabbling in the occult—reading about spiritualism, taking mind-expanding drugs, contacting mediums and tarot cards, flirting with the devil, playing with white magic and casting spells, attempting astral travel, and willingly praying for spirit guides to come in and take them on spiritual adventures—would lead to oppression in every area of their lives, I doubt they would have chosen that path.

Of the two girls who walked out of the dark lord's shadow lands, Tami stopped at the edge of intimacy with Jesus. She received a measure of the Lord's healing embrace but shied away from the radiance of His ongoing presence of love and light. She built her house in a grey place, the realm that Graham Cooke calls in the Foreword to this book, "the shifting shadows of loyalty which people can inhabit when they do not reside in the light, close to the beacon of faithfulness." Ann, however, chose to live in the center of light captivated by the radiance of God's smile—her reality shaped by intimacy with Christ, her life a testimony of the power of the Holy Spirit.

This story illustrates what is happening in families worldwide—light and darkness impact us all. What we choose to attend to ultimately defines our spiritual life and our emotional health. Yet it also illustrates the story of any local church, a family whose individual members attend on any given day to shadows of half-hearted devotion to the God of love, falling into the shifting shadows of loyalty that bind them either to themselves or lead them to collude with the dark lord.

There is a difference between psychic and soulish power, Christian and demonic power, counterfeits and authentic expressions of the Spirit of God moving through an individual. Throughout the ages, light and dark powers have existed, warring against each other for control of individuals, communities, and nations. As a result, personalities fragment under the pressure, neighborhoods deteriorate, and nations crumble. This book attempts to reveal the differences in the sources of supernatural power, the impact of expressions of revelatory and healing in the lives of others, and how you can reach out and minister in authentic supernatural power—the power of the Lord Jesus Christ.

CHAPTER 2

Shifting Shadows of Power

The world is rich in spiritual power. Where does it come from? Is it psychic or latent soulish power at work? Is it God or is it satan? How can you tell the difference? As individuals become increasingly stressed by life events and economics, many feel powerless and out of control. As a result, some pursue power, gravitating toward it either from a desire to be entertained or out of desperate need for control. For others, power meets their needs—these individuals seem divinely appointed to wield power for the good or the ill of others.

As more people access supernatural power—both occult power and authentic power—discernment will be vital in the years to come. Power flows through an individual's personality and character. An individual's soul directs the flow of power no matter what the source. There are Christians who begin using the gifts of the spirit and move in authentic power only to end up in deception. Just as there are occult practitioners who end up surrendering their lives to Jesus then suddenly discover God's authentic power.

In the coming days and years, how can you tell who's got the real power? Satan or Jesus? Psychics or prophets? Sorcerers or healing evangelists? And how can you tell if a Christian is operating in authentic power or soulish power? The marks of power that come from God and from demonic deception are as different as night and day. It is the soul of the person expressing the power that creates the shifting shadows of confusion.

New Creation Power Brokers

Gifts of healing, miracles, visions, and seeing into the supernatural realm seem to have been more commonplace among practitioners of the occult and the New Age movement in past decades. Christians who talked about being overcome by the Spirit of the Lord Jesus Christ, receiving visions, dreams and supernatural healing, were often criticized, regarded as being deceived, and eyed with suspicion—even within the Church. As a result, many believers shut down, learning that it was best to keep their spiritual experiences a secret.

In the 1980s, however, the Charismatic Christian prophetic movement in North America quickly normalized individuals' spiritual experiences and released greater understanding of the richness of biblical accounts of the revelatory nature of God and the supernatural reality of the Kingdom of God. It is for many a Kingdom that is not far off in Heaven, but a Kingdom rapidly breaking into earth by releasing dreams, visions, healings, visitations from angels, miracles, and supernatural experiences to many Christians. It is as if the supernatural is now super-Natural.

Accessing the power of God is no longer just for the power brokers—solo men and women with healing ministries like Aimee Simple McPherson, Kathryn Kuhlman, and Benny Hinn—or televangelists or prophets. A *new creation reality* is becoming mainstream in the Charismatic churches and many ministers are teaching individuals how to access the power and gifts of the Holy Spirit in new ways, using new language. Expressions of Charismatic gifts are no longer about one person mounting a platform to release his or her spiritual gift. The Charismatic gifts are now becoming integrated into every believer's life and being powerfully expressed to others in the workplace, the mission field, and the Church.

According to Canadian evangelist and prophetic minister Patricia King, "As a new creation in Christ we are all able to access healing, visions, and spiritual experiences. They are the new creation realities mentioned in

Second Corinthians 5:17. God wants our spiritual sensitivity awakened. In North America, we are so academic the Lord is trying to break into that orientation and surface the hunger."[1]

King, among other prophetic voices, believes the Church is transitioning into a super-Naturally spiritual time. "Spirituality is one of the greatest commodities in this time as people look for a power that is greater than themselves. Yet, much of the established Western church—both Charismatic and Evangelical—seems afraid of spiritual encounters, organizing their church programs and liturgy to maintain an intellectual approach to faith, an approach that seemingly disregards many of the spiritual experiences contained within the Bible," she says.

The upcoming generation, however, having been wounded by broken families and steeped in popular culture and media promoting the occult, is hungry for authentic power. According to King, "People are now being stirred for a fresh touch of God, especially the unsaved. They are not hungry for institutionalized religion, they are hungry for encounters with God. As a result, much of the activity of the Holy Spirit will be found outside the walls of the church today."

We are seeing a younger generation of Christians encountering God and purposing to take His presence and power outside the confines of the church and into the streets. They are embracing the true Kingdom power and receiving training in a proliferation of ministry schools held in churches and conference settings across the nation. As a result they are fast becoming the first generation to be equipped to release the fullness of the gifts of the Holy Spirit wherever they go—rather than being confined to an expression of an occasional gift of the Spirit.[2]

Leaders such as John Arnott in Toronto, Canada; Mike Bickle in Kansas City, Missouri; Mahesh Chavda in Charlotte, North Carolina; Randy Clark in Harrisburg, Pennsylvania; David Crone in Vacaville, California; Jim Goll in Franklin, Tennessee; Rick Joyner in Charlotte, North Carolina; and Bill Johnson, and Kris Vallotton in Redding, California host ministry schools, conferences and mission trips that are inciting youth to rebel against secular society and enter into new creation realities and authentic power. They are also inflaming the godly jealousy of their elders who have longed to experience the ever-present, supernatural realm of the Kingdom of God through visions, spiritual encounters, and power to heal that comes so readily to youths. Many of these elders have participated in past Charismatic movements and settled into the routines of life, losing vision in the process. They, too, are being stirred to access the presence and power of God alongside the youths, forming a renewed, intergenerational move of God. They are tapping into the new creation realities and running with both the Word of God and the Spirit of God, taking risks and acting on their faith.

Demonic Power Brokers

Psychics, sorcerers, and mediums have a lot in common with many Christians exhibiting revelatory power and the gifts of healing. They offer words of encouragement, insight into the future, reflections of the past or present, and they reveal secrets and predict future events. When it comes down to promoting popular, politically-correct culture, the one with the most entertainment value and who is the least offensive wins.

With demonic power, a man touches the foreheads of several people standing in line and watches briefly, as they crumble to the ground. A woman stares over the shoulder of the one she is addressing and sees spirits of the dead talking to her, imparting knowledge only they know. A young man stands atop a statue in New York City for days, supernaturally unflinching, descending only to continue wowing people on the street with magic tricks never before seen.

Some people channel spirits that assume control of their bodies and speak through their mouths in an altered voice bringing comfort, encouragement, easing their listener's minds from grief, or releasing direction to them. They are all demonic power brokers—imitating the power of the Holy Spirit but denying the deity, death, and resurrection of Jesus Christ. As a result of the shifting shadows flitting across the demonic power brokers' stage, many viewers become entranced and fooled by the demonstrations of power unfolding before them.

However, despite the rise in popularity of demonic power brokers, we are seeing a growing number of Christians and non-Christians who see through the darkness and recognize that not all power is authentic power—only the power that is released through the authority of the Lord Jesus Christ is real. We are also seeing people renounce their loyalty to the dark lord on his dark throne, step out of the shadows of confusion, and become incredible new creation power brokers shortly after conversion.

From Sorcerer to Prophet

Ian Clayton, a New Zealand prophet and father of four, is a man who found himself seemingly chosen by the demonic realm to become a great occult leader. Yet God had other plans, shifting the shadows of power aside to reveal Himself and lead Ian into an entirely different realm of grace. His story illustrates the powers of the occult as well as the ability of light to overcome the darkness in an individual's life, shifting them out of the shadows until they enter into authentic power and supernatural experiences initiated by the Holy Spirit.[3]

Psychics claim that the ability to see and move in the supernatural is often inherited and can trace the lineage of relatives who moved in psychic power for generations past. In Ian's case, the generational lines seemed to offer two distinct destinies for Ian's spiritual gifts. On his mother's side of the family is a line of Jewish and Christian believers. One great grandfather was counted among the original Quakers in Africa. During the mid-1800s, another great grandfather experienced the Welch revival.

His father's side of the family was exactly the opposite. His father was the head of the spiritualist church in Africa. His family lineage included free masons, Rosicrucian's, and those with claims to other occult involvement.

It wasn't long before the two warring destinies manifested in Ian's life as power reached out and touched him at an early age. As a child, Ian would see visions of Jesus and angels. Eventually, his father took him to the spiritualist church and things began to change. The dark side aggressively pursued Ian, shifted him into the shadows, and lured him into the occult.

At age 12, his growing awareness of God led him to the Bible and he started reading it from the beginning. Halfway through Deuteronomy he decided that it was full of rules and regulations and didn't want anything to do with it. Just as he shut the Bible he heard a voice say, "Put your hand on top of table and pick table up." Ian put his hand flat on the table top and it rose, sideways off the floor.

"It was an amazing power rush," Ian explained. "Suddenly, I walked in power."

Spirits started materializing at night and taught Ian how to do things such as astral travel and psychic healing, pendulum diagnosis, use of herbs in healing and in gaining power, and the power of demons in the spirit world. As the lessons continued, people grew frightened of Ian's power. Many would talk about the headaches they got after being around him—headaches Ian attributes to the demonic resonance of the spirit force around his life. Meanwhile, signs and wonders manifested in Ian's life much to his surprise and others' shock.

"I would put my hand out and it would go into the wall—not up against it," he said. By age 17, Ian was frightened of his own power and turned into an introvert attempting to shelter himself from others because of the phenomena that would occur.

The power then transitioned him into deeper realms of a supernatural world. "A generational sentinel appeared as a jaguar then became a man who taught me for a year about issues of sorcery and how to make and destroy things," Ian said. "I thought I would use this power for the good of others without realizing the source was evil and would actually release demons into their lives. I didn't know this until I was born again."

According to Ian, the spirits taught him to become a psychic healer and he would lay hands on a body and take out the bits that were diseased. He could heal and he could kill with the same power that resided within him. "The moment I touched their flesh they submitted to the demon in my life. When I got angry at somebody I would release spirits and the people either were killed or became sick. At one point, my father got sick and my mother ended up in hospital because of my cursing them."

Eventually, Ian met a woman who would become his wife, and she gradually grew accustomed to the strange nocturnal visitations Ian received from spirits, believing that Ian's spiritual giftedness was destined to help many people. However, one of her college instructors challenged her beliefs during an after-class discussion when he opened the Bible and read a Scripture about consulting with demons being an abomination to God. Near the end of the discussion, he invited them over to his house for a barbecue.

She brought the Bible home to Ian and everything inside of him reacted. One night the sentinel appeared to him and tried to dissuade him from attending the dinner. But something else, some other part of his family lineage, drew him closer to the source of authentic power and his ultimate destiny.

They attended the dinner and adjourned to another room for worship and Bible study. "Suddenly, this thing came through the roof and descended into the room. It was so beyond what I had ever seen. As this cloud came down into the room I wanted to get away and ended up on the floor. I looked at this girl's face of abandoned love worshiping this thing that came into the room and realized that what I wanted all my life was to be loved, not used. As soon as she stopped worshiping the cloud left."

His girlfriend accepted the Lord and began weeping as she felt God healing her body and her emotions. Ian then asked Jesus into his life. The small group of believers went to Ian's house to pray over the rooms and cleanse it from the demonic. They also encouraged him to throw away all his occult objects. "They said to me, 'You've confessed Jesus as Savior; now you need to confess Him as your Lord.' The moment I did that it felt like a sword went right into my heart and I began to see the death, destruction, chaos, and all that what was using me; and I sat on the floor and wept.

"For me to get free I had to own what I had done. Satan knew that if I came into my destiny as a son of God, I would become his worst nightmare."

It took time for Ian to disentangle from demonic influences and power. His salvation initiated a two-year process of healing and deliverance in his life. The last thing to go was the sentinel—smaller demons were easily cast out. "I realized that the sentinel was an imitation of the Holy Spirit, a trespasser who had no right to come in and teach me and shut my life down," Ian said.

"When I got delivered, the inside of my heart tore as I felt it claw its way out. Afterward, for the first time since age 12, the grass was green. I heard the birds singing and the sky was blue. The deliverance began a hatred of anything to do with the demonic."

Over the years, Ian grew in his faith and in the ability to discern the shifting shadows of power that infiltrate society. His openness to the spiritual realm enabled him to readily recognize the authentic power of the Holy Spirit—power characterized by life rather than destruction—and experience the supernatural Kingdom of God.

Rather than initiating astral travel as he learned to do through the help of spirit guides, he walks with the Father of Light and His Son, Jesus Christ, discovering new realms of Heaven and insights into the supernatural. Rather than wallowing in depression and anger, he is a joyful person, full of light and exuberant with life. Rather than being a servant of the demonic, he is a servant of the Lord with a growing international reputation as a prophet who not only understands the spirit realm but teaches others how to access the power of God and enter the revelatory realms of God's Kingdom—rather than access the revelation of the occult.

Ian Clayton is a man who has experienced not only the counterfeit powers of satan, but authentic power of God. Everything he had done through occult power he has also experienced through authentic power...and more. He believes that when Jesus Christ told His disciples that they will accomplish greater works and miracles than He, it should be taken literally. Christians operating in the authentic power of the Holy Spirit, can heal the sick, raise the dead, walk on water, dematerialize and walk through a crowd (or walls for that matter), see into both the realm of Heaven and satan's dominion, and take authority over all of the enemy's work. Having walked on both sides of the fence, Ian believes that God's authentic power is greater. He is a New Creation Power Broker experiencing things most Christians cannot imagine—fourth dimension miracles that transcend our current knowledge of the laws of physics.

The Coming Showdown—A Clash of Supernatural Powers

As New Creation Power Brokers increase within the Church, so do the demonic counterfeits.

34

Since the fall of Adam and the ousting of lucifer from Heaven, lucifer has been organizing his forces, trying to regain his seat of power and becoming the ultimate enemy of the people of God. He set all in motion against the people of God, trying to sway them over to his side, luring them in, seducing them with the smooth lies of promise of a future filled with all the longings of their hearts. The adversary made repeated attempts to destroy God's people—the Israelites—coming against her priests and prophets, stirring up deceiving spirits trying to sway the elect into crossing over to his side. And when they continued to worship God, his anger lashed out and a bloodbath ensued.

Then came Jesus Christ who triumphed over lucifer by becoming the ultimate sacrifice for the people of God, expanding the Kingdom rule and reign of God and inviting all who believe in Jesus as their Savior to become the children of God. The enemy was further enraged and set into motion a counter-attack. He continues to summon all of his might against both the Israelites, Christians, and those who respond to the love of Christ, trying to cut them off and keep them from knowing the fullness of Christ, His power, and the vast resources of His Kingdom.

Hordes of demonic spirits have been let loose in every culture. They counterfeit the power of God in hopes of luring unsuspecting people into a head nest of lies and deception. They are the gods of this age and come in the guise of occult power. Children's games, videos, and computer programs are rife with occult images. Adult television, movies, and Internet preoccupations also reveal a technological twist on an ancient game, as the adversary seeks to lure our culture into deeper encounters with the archetypal gods of Baal and Asthoreh—gods that lead to varying degrees of occult practices and sexual deviation.

Throughout history, God has always revealed His power during society's darkest hours. There have been repeated showdowns against the gods of the ages, the prophets of the Baals, the enemies of the Church and the enemies of Israel. As a result of revelations of the authentic power of God, many people given over to occult practices either walk away from their practices, die, or seek to purchase the power of God so that they can use it for their own prosperity.

The Bible contains several stories about people in the occult suddenly recognizing that their power pales in comparison to the power of God. Some decided to stop competing or imitating the authentic power of God and walked away, realizing that they could go no further. Others were overcome by fear when they realized that they went beyond the limits of their own power and God showed up (much to their surprise). Still others sought to obtain the pure undefiled power resident in God's prophets and believers and purchase it, if they could, in hopes of making a profit on that power. These prophets, mediums, and sorcerers released demonic signs and wonders that looked so much like what God could do that many people opted to follow them rather than God.

Historic Showdowns

Moses tossed his staff a few feet away from his feet, watching as it twisted in mid air, became fluid, and fell to the floor no longer a rigid length of wood but a writhing snake. Alchemy. A mere magician's trick—changing one form of matter into another. Several sorcerers stood by confident that they too possessed the power to throw down their staffs and create a nest of snakes. One by one they tossed their staffs to the ground until the floor was awash in snakes. Suddenly, one snake drew back into a coil, raised its head high and struck at the snake closest by, devouring it quickly before winding its way to the next snake. By the end of the hour, Moses' snake had consumed the sorcerers' snakes. Its belly full, it stretched out full length on the floor and shapeshifted back into the form of a staff.[4]

The sorcerers imitated almost every trick Moses had up his sleeve. Moses launched a plague and the sorcerers, attempting to one up Moses, ironically added their power to the purpose of God and extended the plague, duplicating it in other regions of Egypt. In the end, however, they admitted that they could go no further. They had come to the end of their ability to imitate God's power and turned and walked away.

Saul, devastated in heart and spirit, longed for a word from the prophet Samuel who had anointed him king in the first place. The problem: Samuel was dead. God didn't seem to be speaking with Saul in his hour of need. No other prophets nearby held any words of comfort for Saul. He felt alone, abandoned, afraid of the days to come. In the absence of any other prophets in the area, he sought out a medium, hoping she would channel the spirit of Samuel. She dwelt in a cave, hiding her profession because Saul had condemned mediums and spiritists to death. So, she was dubious at first to grant Saul an audience; but she went ahead because she did not recognize that it was Saul who stood before her.

She sat back, closed her eyes, spoke a few unintelligible words of incantation, calling out to the spirit of Samuel, hoping that his familiar spirit would show up, a spirit that could, at best, imitate Samuel's voice and knew intimate details of Samuel's life. Suddenly, she felt the presence of another in the cave. Out of the darkness, a figure emerged. She gasped and cried out in shock. It wasn't the familiar spirit of Samuel. It was Samuel himself, raised from the dead. Then she realized Saul was her client and she became very afraid.[5]

Elijah felt like the time was right. The land and the people had suffered enough from drought and famine. It was time to release the sound of the coming of rain. But first, he had to recapture the hearts of the people of God and make them realize that God was alive and powerful, more powerful than the false prophets who bowed the knee to the Baals. The Baals had already failed to provide rain, failed to prosper the land and make it fertile. No matter how much they sacrificed, danced, prayed, and gave themselves over to increasing debauchery, the Baals failed to come through for the people. It was time to reveal the power of God. Perhaps the people would listen now that they were getting desperate.[6]

Elijah called for a showdown on Mount Carmel. One prophet of God against hundreds of prophets of Baal. The showdown would prove who's got the power—God or the false gods.

He prepared an altar and poured water over the sticks until they were saturated. There would be no lighter fluid, nothing to jump-start the fire or even light it by using natural means. Who would light the fire—God or Baal? The prophets of Baal did everything they could to get the fire going. They danced, called out to their gods, and slashed themselves until their blood splattered the dust. For hours on end they wailed and waited for Baal to come through and show his power. Elijah patiently waited. Every once in awhile he taunted them just as they had taunted him in the past, mocking the true prophets of God. Slowly, the people warmed to Elijah, their hearts turning toward all that he stood for. Elijah seemed so confident that the people's faith increased as their fears that God had abandoned them abated.

"If God is God, then follow Him!" Elijah pleaded with the people—not the people given over to the world system of Baal in that day, but his own people, the children of God, God's chosen, the church of that day. "But if Baal be god then follow him. Choose you this day whom you will serve."

Elijah lifted his eyes to Heaven and the prophets of Baal dropped to the ground exhausted from their efforts to entreat their gods. The fire of God crackled from Heaven to earth, consuming not only the sacrifice that lay on the altar but burning so hot that it consumed the altar itself—a nuclear blast from Heaven. And the people grew very afraid. They realized that God is alive and present, that God is the God of authentic power. Great anger rose up in them as they also realized how deceived and frightened they had become during the years of Jezebel's reign of terror, under the misguidance of prophets who offered only self-abuse and destruction, false hopes, and unreality. And in that anger, boldness arose. They sided with Elijah, rose up as a people, and destroyed the false prophets.

One of the most interesting encounters between a prophet/apostle and a sorcerer happened in the New Testament Book of Acts. A sorcerer drew the attention of the people with his magic tricks, his predictions, the way he touched people, and their shrieks of delight when they realized that they were healed. The people loved him. But then another came their way, an apostle who had been with Jesus. He too touched the people and they were healed. And yet he offered the people something more, some power that caused them to speak in other languages, and become overwhelmed as they felt the love and power of God moving in their lives. Even the sorcerer tasted of that power and knew it was good; so good that it intoxicated him. And he wanted more. He wanted it so badly that he went up to the apostle and asked how much it would cost him to purchase that anointing of power. He knew that his own power of sorcery was nothing in comparison.[7]

The apostle set him straight. God's power was not for sale. It was (and still is) a gift from God to those who inherited salvation and a Kingdom that was not of this world. God, it seemed, was no longer in the Old Testament mode of slaying the prophets of Baal, sorcerers, mediums, spiritists, alchemists, and diviners. Instead, God wanted to release His authentic power to seek and save all of the lost—including those who had become entranced by occult power and lured into the kingdom of darkness. Whereas the showdowns of the Old Testament often turned into bloodbaths, the showdowns of the New are revelations of the power of God's love.

We may be entering a time in history when another showdown with the prophets of Baal is imminent. What will this encounter look like? Will the showdown occur inside the Church or out in the world, on the streets complete with miraculous displays of power? Today's prophets have much to say on the topic. And they all seem to agree on one thing—the showdown is already happening in our midst and it's going to get weirder than anything we've seen or read. But first of all, a showdown must occur within ourselves as we step out of the shifting shadows of confusion regarding the source of supernatural power operating in individual lives and step into our callings as Christians to release the presence and power of God wherever we go.

Discerning the Source of Supernatural Power

Discerning the source, or origin, of supernatural displays of power is not difficult. Anyone moving in revelatory, supernatural power will become like the one they behold. The more surrendered a person becomes to the source of the power, the more purely it reveals itself. Testimonies included later in this book reveal that one given over to the demonic will receive and express increasingly destructive power resulting in personalities that fragment under the weight of oppression. One given over to the Holy Spirit will receive and express increasingly authentic power resulting in a personality and life characterized by love, peace, and joy. Soulish power is merely a mixture of shadows originating in a person's mind.

There are specific marks that characterize the origins or source of supernatural power expressed through individuals. Richard Foster details seven marks of God's authentic power in his book *The Challenge of the Disciplined Life*. They include: love, humility, restraint, joy, vulnerability, submission, and freedom from control. [8]

If that is to be our guide for discerning the source of God's power, then the marks of power that proceed from the occult and demonic realm would involve the exact opposite characteristics. They would include: hate, pride, unbridled displays of power, depression, jealousy, inability to relate to others or allow others to speak into their lives, and a desire to control others.

Soulish power—that which originates from a person's state of mind and heart—expresses itself with a variety of mixed markers. Unhealed, unaffirmed people tend to exercise their soulish power to manipulate people and events to compensate for an overwhelming sense of their own powerlessness. Because they have no strong sense of identity or core self rooted in relationship with Jesus Christ, they attempt to acquire an external derivation of significance. As a result, when they express the spiritual gifts, the recipients may feel tainted by the residue of soulish imprints. One receiving a prophetic word originating in another's soul power may feel more like the word is mere manipulation or flattery, a put down or a power trip. The laying on of hands for healing may also feel like a power trip drawing attention not to the healing power and presence of Jesus Christ and His atonement, but to the presence of the one praying.

For some, expressing soulish power is part of the process of normal spiritual growth and personal healing. A healthy process leads them to become secure in setting boundaries with others rather than attempting to control others and involves repeated encounters with the healing presence of Jesus Christ. An unhealthy process drives them into the occult realm and their minds become playgrounds for the antics of the demonic.

Attempts to harness and express power that originate in the soul are but one extreme. The other extreme involves those who seek power based on narcissistic desire. To obtain spiritual power for the glorification of self is to align oneself with the demonic. Lucifer is the ultimate narcissist.

The marks of power that come from God are the marks of a healthy personality as well as a mature Christian who is secure in God's love. When authentic power works deeply in the lives of individuals releasing healing into their wounds, they can release it more purely to others through words of knowledge, prophesies, miracles, and healings that relate the heart of a loving God. Since most of us need progressive healing and sanctification and are not free from expressions of hate, pride, jealousy, and depression how can we determine the origins of power that flow through mere humans?

First, we need to recognize that soul power is not entirely bad. Our life experiences (good and bad), personalities, and giftedness are given to us for a reason—to co-labor with God as we enter into our destinies. God gives us a vision but we have a role to play in working that out. Soul power rooted in God's love and understanding of the particular destiny and vision given to each individual tempers our human nature on any given bad day. Soul power, working under submission to God's power, also gets the work done. We release the power of God through our soul, or mindful action, and the marks of power will correspondingly bear the marks of our personality. God, having given you a unique personality, loves the way you express Him.

Second, no matter what our state of heart and mind, our level of maturity or brokenness, the imprint of soulish origins fades when overshadowed by the anointing of the Holy Spirit. God's loving presence can move through the youngest child or most immature and unhealed adult to accomplish His will. His power is made perfect in our weakness.

Releasing God's Authentic Power

Our challenge and responsibility is not to move in power but to move in the presence of God...to walk in intimate relationship with the one who releases His anointing through us. We become like the one we behold and worship. By seeking to draw closer to the God of power we become increasingly more like Him. The marks of power that come from God are also reflections of His nature. The more we seek the God of authentic power, the purer His anointing will flow through us. The more we seek the god of self and occult power, the more fragmented our personalities and lives are destined to become.

41

Those who desire to move in God's authentic anointing, releasing the power of God to seek and save the lost, demonstrate that the Kingdom of God is near. They invite others to glimpse a testimony of Jesus—who is the same yesterday, today and forever—and they exhibit certain characteristics. Those characteristics mark the power broker as one who walks intimately with Jesus, beholding His presence, accepting His nature. The marks of authentic power, according to Richard Foster, are best defined as:

Love

Love uses power for the good of others rather than to advance one's own reputation. It calls attention to the lover of our souls, the God of love, and gives Christ all the praise and glory.

Humility

Humility recognizes that God's power is a gift to be used under control, submitted to the will of God rather than the will of self, and submitted to others who can teach us how to wield the power of God appropriately.

Restraint

Restraint refuses to use power to validate one's reputation, conform to the desires of others, dispel unbelief, or release others into their gifts and callings before God's ordained time. Jesus moved in power, healing and delivering everyone in some settings. Yet He restrained Himself from healing, raising the dead, or speaking prophetically during other times.

Joy

Joy gives evidence to the nearness of God's presence for in His presence is fullness of joy—despite the surrounding darkness. The one who releases power from a joyful heart is truly aware that Christ's blood triumphs over every work of the enemy.

Vulnerability

Vulnerability realizes that power does not give one the right to dominate others or to control them. Nor is a display of power evidence of the strength of the power broker—for God's authentic power is made perfect in our weakness.

Submission

Submission accepts the leadership of Christ and cooperation with the authority of others who offer access to wisdom, guidance and encouragement in the development of the gifts of the Holy Spirit that comes forth with power.

Freedom

Freedom never uses power to control or exploit people in extreme situations. Jesus freely healed and delivered and fed the masses who, in gratitude, would have done whatever He wished—including storming the Jewish and Roman authorities to make Christ an earthly king. He strove not to manipulate or control them, or coerce them into following Him, but empowered them to become themselves.

Habitations of the Spirit

We all run the risk of self-delusion and self-destruction. In the following chapters, you will notice that failure to receive God's love and enter into deep relationship with the person of Jesus Christ, the source of authentic power, will ultimately result in tainted displays of power that may lead to either delusion or self-destruction. Failure to embrace the person and the authentic power of the Holy Spirit may also result in self-delusion.

Mahesh Chavda, internationally known minister and forerunner of today's Charismatic healing movement, warns in his book, *The Hidden Power of the Blood of Jesus*: "God intends for us to be habitations for His Spirit. If we reject the Holy Spirit, nothing is left except the spirit of the enemy."[9]

The Second Great Awakening, led by Charles Finney, opened a dimensional gateway of the spirit realm that led many into great encounters with the Holy Spirit and salvation. Out of the revival emerged new ways of preaching, a breaking of religious structures of thought and liturgy, and a release of social justice and the beginnings of racial and gender equality. It paved the way for our modern Charismatic and Pentecostal movement.

However, the Second Great Awakening also paved the way for counterfeit manifestations of the spirit world that led many into a growing interest in spiritualism. Into the spiritual void left by the waning revival, the modern spiritualist and occult revival was born. Those who rejected the Holy Spirit eventually gave themselves over to either intellectualism, ardent Calvinism, apathy, or demonic spirits enticing them into the shadows of spiritualism.

History reveals that those who press into the realm of the Kingdom of God dare not stop but continue to go from glory to glory, expressing the authentic power of the Holy Spirit until the end of this age…an age that will eventually culminate in a great clash of powers. Christians must choose whom they will serve, take their place in the plan of God for this present day, and release Heaven on earth—or nothing will be left but one vast habitation of the enemy.

ENDNOTES

1. Quotes and information about Patricia King cited in this chapter are derived from a telephone interview. King is noted for her ministry of "prophetic evangelism" and has written several books on the topic. Originally based in Kelowna, Canada, her ministry base has moved to Arizona. For more information see her Website at www.extreme-prophetic.com.

2. The varieties of the gifts of the Holy Spirit are found in First Corinthians, chapter 12. Although in our generation John Wimber popularized the teachings that all the gifts of the Spirit can be expressed through one person according to the will of the Lord and the need at hand, many churches and ministries have still emphasized the dominance of one or another gifting being activated in a person's life for purposes of ministering to others. Current ministry schools seem to be focusing on activation of all the gifts of the Holy Spirit moving through an individual.

3. Quotes and information about Ian Clayton cited in this chapter are derived from a telephone interview. Clayton may be contacted through Steve Trullinger's ministry. For more information see Trullinger's Website at www.fatherstouch.org.

4. Exodus, chapters 7-10.

5. 1 Samuel 2.

6. 1 Kings 18.

7. Acts 8:9-25.

8. Richard J. Foster, *The Challenge of the Disciplined Life*. (New York: HarperCollins Publishers, 1985), 201-207.

9. Mahesh Chavda, *The Hidden Power of the Blood of Jesus*. (Shippensburg, PA: Destiny Image Publishers, 2004), 105. Mahesh and Bonnie Chavda are prolific authors and power brokers of the Holy Spirit. For more information see their Website at: www.maheshchavda.com.

CHAPTER 3

Revelatory Power of Psychics and Mediums

Occult beliefs and themes appear to be so imbedded in modern society that it seems an impossible task to separate them. In fact, many naïve Christians also buy into those beliefs, consult the occasional psychic or Tarot card reader, focus on astrology, and become confused, believing that all power is God's power. But is it? How can you tell whether psychic power comes from God? Sometimes, you can't. Where does their revelatory power come from? That, too, is not simple to discern.

Why are so many people in every generation gravitating toward the occult? The pressure to find some solace after heart-wrenching life events and the desire to know what lies ahead propels many into the arms of psychic readers and mediums. Eventually, they discover that they had either consulted charlatans or gifted psychics who transmitted more than they bargained for.

According to Christian prophet John Paul Jackson in an article posted on his Streams Ministries Website,

"Our culture today is obsessed with witchcraft, astrology, necromancy, sorcery, and spiritism. We live in a time when the lost, often unwittingly, 'exchange the truth of God for the lie' (Romans 1:25 NKJV). Scripture foretold of this time: 'For false christs and false prophets will rise and show signs and wonders to deceive, if possible, even the elect' (Mark 13:22 NKJV).

"Sadly, it is often people who are at their lowest point who are the most vulnerable to this deception. As time marches on, the visibility of psychics and occult practitioners will grow. As times crescendo toward instability, there will be an increased demand to know what lies ahead. Consequently, people will look to either the occult or to God for the answers."[1]

Kris Vallotton, associate pastor and prophetic minister of Bethel Church in Redding California, has had many encounters with psychics who flock to Northern California's diverse New Age climate. He believes that many who gravitated toward the occult were tormented or traumatized when they were children and were open to any spiritual experience that offered them power. As they enter deeper into occult-based revelation, they eventually realize that the spirits that initially enticed them with love and peace transformed into entities that were out to control and torment. "The goal of every demonic spirit is to kill, steal, and destroy and they will get into someone's life through any means. Once they get in you can't get them out unless you have Jesus," he said, and related the following story.[2]

Flying home from a conference, Kris and his wife found themselves sitting next to a woman who looked like an ordinary, everyday housewife. "She was acting normal but I could feel this whole spiritual thing surrounding her that felt like a suicidal entity on her."

The woman picked up a book with Asian writing on the cover and Kris, by this time convinced that the seating arrangements on this flight were a divine appointment, asked her what the book was about. She replied that she was a Buddhist; the book was about Buddhism. She also told him that she was trained as a psychic by the psychic network.

"I leaned over to her and said, 'So you're a psychic huh? That spirit guide you have is a demon and it's trying to kill you."

She tried to ignore him and held the book closer to her face pretending to read. But Kris, gaining more prophetic insight into the woman's life wouldn't let up and said, "Hey, you know why you let that demon in your life when you were a little girl? Because you were molested when you were about 8 years old."

The book lowered from her face and she replied, "You are freaking me out."

Then Kris asked her who John was.

Her voice grew softer as she told him that John was her uncle, the man who molested her.

"God told me to ask you about the car accident," he continued.

"Which accident? I've been in three accidents in the last 18 months. When the spirit guide talks to me, I rear end people."

"It's trying to kill you and you need to be delivered," Kris replied.

After a bit more conversation, the woman tried ignoring Kris again and resumed reading her book. She flipped through several pages and stopped. Then, she flipped through some more pages and stopped to read, clearly becoming anxious. Suddenly, she threw the book on the floor of the plane saying, "This is freaking me out." She then picked up the book and showed it to Kris, randomly pointing out on various pages where the author stated in various ways—"some people need to be delivered because they are tormented by evil spirits."

Kris gently asked if he could pray for her. After overcoming her reluctance, he simply prayed, "Holy Spirit, show her that you're real, that you love her, and that she is being deceived."

The woman appeared to fall asleep for about 20 minutes. Then she opened her eyes looked at Kris and said, "It's peaceful in here." Tears pooled in her eyes as she continued, "I haven't had peace since I was a little girl."

In the process of meeting the Prince of Peace (Isaiah 9:6) she discovered that she had been leaning on the devourer (1 Peter 5:8).

The Origins of Psychic Popularity

Madame Helen Blavatsky, born in Russia in 1831, is known as the "mother of the modern spiritualist movement," popularizing mediumistic and psychic powers and merging world religions into what is the foundation of the modern New Age movement in America.

She claimed to have been born with considerable psychic powers and had childhood visions of a tall Hindu who eventually materialized in Hyde Park and became her guru and advisor. She married at the age of 16 and soon after left her 40-year-old husband, working a variety of odd jobs including a stint as a bareback rider in the circus and séance assistant. Traveling throughout the world, Blavatsky studied Eastern religious teachings and philosophies in India and the Himalayas, eventually making her way back to the U.S. in 1873, at the height of the spiritualist fad sweeping the nation at that time.

While in Vermont, Blavatsky associated with the Eddy brothers who displayed brazen psychic powers complete with demonstrations of flying furniture and musical spirits, manifestations that magician Harry Houdini would later claim devoid of mystic power and mere magic. Blavatsky came up with a few tricks of her own—channeling spirits and sending flowers and otherworldly missives raining down on her audience. It was there she met Henry Steel Olcott. Olcott, along with other newspaper correspondents eager to please an audience hungry for bizarre supernatural tales, made her a frequent subject for his articles. Together, they founded the Theosophical Society in New York City in September 1875.

Oddly enough, the Theosophical Society was founded in the same area of New York City where Christian revivalist Charles Finney lived from 1830 through 1831, the peak years of The Second Great Awakening. Prayer meetings were crowded almost every night. Conversions and confessions of sin were frequent. Demonstrations of the power of the Holy Spirit amazed those who attended the meetings. Finney's new approach to evangelism resulted in the belief that "Heaven on earth" was possible; and the revival movement led to many secular reform movements including abolition, temperance, public education, philanthropic endeavors, and the liberation of women who were encouraged to become missionaries and lay preachers.

The societal changes emerging from the Second Great Awakening unwittingly set the stage for nations to be open to spiritual power, open to laity rather than solo ministers preaching and ministering in power, and open to something other than a staid, Calvinist belief and the structure of liturgical church services.

By the 1850s, the Great Awakening religious fervor had died down. Many Victorians began rejecting conventional religion and spiritualism flowed into the spiritual void of America and Europe. The religious climate of America had been primed to experience increasing spiritual power but lacked a cohesive structure to sustain either a revival of Christianity or a revival of occult mysticism.

By 1880, spiritist's parlor tricks like table lifting, mysterious tapping, channeling the voice of the dead, and levitation lost their entertainment value. Blavatsky and Olcott moved to India and established a Theosophical headquarters there until her psychic abilities and manifestations were discredited by both the Indian "Masters" and the British Society for Psychical Research. [The BSPS and its American counterpart (American Society for Psychical Research) have attracted some brilliant leaders in arts and sciences who "investigate" the paranormal usually from a point of view sympathetic to Theosophical beliefs. Counted among the early leaders are 12 Nobel prizewinners, Fellows of the Royal Society, psychologists William James, Carl Jung, and Sigmund Freud, and writers such as Robert Louis Stevenson, Mark Twain and Walt Whitman.]

However, Blavatsky was not deterred and merely moved to England and launched into writing her voluminous works, upon which the foundation of the Theosophical society still rests.

Blavatsky tried to disentangle herself from occult labels that connoted an antichristian bias and a bent toward evil and developed a theoretical framework borrowed from Hindu mysticism, the Jewish cabala, myths of Atlantis, and European neoplatonism—all wrapped up in one Gnostic package. Her writings offered the world a systematic, quasi-academic approach to the study of paranormal phenomena and made spiritualism intellectually appealing. She established the foundation upon which all occult mysticism and 20th-century expressions of New Age practices have built their particular kingdoms.

51

The term "theosophy" is derived from the Greek words *theos*, meaning God, and *sophia*, meaning wisdom. True Theosophists hold that the divine higher self of every mortal man is of the same essence of the gods. Prove the soul of man by its wondrous powers and you have proved God. In short, man can not only be god but *is* god. Karma and reincarnation are part of their foundational beliefs, but they believe we do not regress back into animals after we die. Instead, they believe that people review their past and rest for awhile before reincarnating into successive lives. Pagan religions and worship of the earth, the sun, solstices, and nature rites are also included in her writings. To Theosophists, the religions of the world are branches on the tree whose trunk is the one ancient—once universal—wisdom religion. Periodically, great teachers (Buddha, Jesus, Dali Lama, etc.) come among us to help us on our evolutionary path. Each creating another branch on the tree.

The fundamental principles of Theosophy are: to form a universal brotherhood of humanity, encourage the study of comparative religion, philosophy and science, and to investigate unexplained laws of nature and the powers latent in humans. Much of the foundational belief system hinges on the survival of consciousness after death, giving rise to the popularity of those psychics who can contact the dead, psychics who can prove their theories.

Tapping into the higher self and reaching into other places of existence seemed to attract those who sought to develop their paranormal faculties. Suddenly the quest for power and control over life became accessible to those who would be gods through exercising the "latent power" in all humans. It is this Theosophical foundation that undergirds today's New Age teachings, Wiccan and pagan religions, and development of occult-related games, children's books, classic literature, and modern television programs.

How Psychics and Mediums Access Revelatory Power

Strangely, the teachings about all humans having a latent ability to manifest signs and wonders, channel spirits from the dead, see visions, supernaturally heal the sick, move objects telepathically, astral travel, and all the other mystical manifestations, are not confined to psychics and modern expressions of theosophy. What is the difference between the origins of psychic power and how can you tell if someone is accessing the power of God, the power of their soul, or demonic power?

Psychic researchers have long claimed that man is capable of training himself to experience increasing abilities of clairvoyance (the ability to see distant or hidden objects), telepathy (ability to transfer thoughts), precognition (ability to see future events), and psychokinesis (ability to manipulate objects mentally).

Many Christians believe that Adam, original man, had unlimited cognitive and paranormal abilities. Given his direct access to God and his capacity to manage a vast garden and name all of the animals, they reason that he must have commanded an unlimited memory, be able to see remote places and events mentally, and teleport himself to other places, among other powers.

After the fall and Adam was booted out of the garden, many believe that those mental powers were removed from humans or they lapsed into dormancy. Fallen angels and creatures like demons, however, retained the ability to counterfeit miracles and power.

Christian author Watchman Nee in his book *The Latent Power of the Soul*, wrote that he believed that many of Adam's original capabilities remain buried deep in our minds. As generations passed, Adam's spiritual and cognitive power became a latent force in our lives. Yet it is not a power to be tapped into. According to Nee, "The work of the devil nowadays is to stir up man's soul [in order] to release this latent power within it as a deception for spiritual power."[3]

Nee believes that God invites us to call on the power of the Holy Spirit rather than draw upon our own soul power. The enemy, satan, hopes to substitute realities that call for man to rely on soul power as a deceptive alternative to the power of the Holy Spirit.

The draw toward power then, is a draw toward one of two sources of power—either God's power or satan's power. The mind of man is therefore neutral until swayed into exercising and developing the power of one's soul through demonic influence or reaching out for the power of the Holy Spirit.

Modern brain imagery and research into the inner workings of the brain suggest that we are capable of forming new neural pathways in response to stimuli. In other words, we learn as we go forward rather than tapping into ancient or latent neural paths. We become like the one we behold. Demonic influence or Holy Spirit power encounters establish new thought processes, memories, and ways of accessing spiritual power as we are exposed to new stimuli.

Patricia King, a prophet whose ministry teaches people how to grow in their revelatory insight and understanding of the Kingdom of Heaven, offers an explanation of the difference between the power of the soul or mind, and the difference between accessing the power of God and demonic.

> "The big issue is source. A psychic is either trusting in their own psyche or in demonic power. Their own minds can pick up energy in the mindwave. They don't necessarily have to have a demon feeding them information. Business people get a read on others all of the time. When I was nursing I could get an intuitive sense of when people were in cardiac arrest.
>
> "The demonic is another source...a false source. Anything to do with spiritual activity [using their own psyche or demonic power] is a forbidden practice in Scripture. In Genesis 1, God gave man stewardship over the natural realm—not the endorsement to start manipulating the spiritual realm. When you go into unseen realms outside the operation of Christ you are operating in witchcraft. If the source is outside Jesus it is a forbidden practice."[4]

The Marks of Demonic Revelation

Psychics want to come across as loving and as offering their gift for the good of the world. In many cases however, their love actually projects manipulation and control, preys on vulnerability and offers a different spiritual message than offered by the God of authentic power and love.

Teachings common to psychic practitioners tend to confuse those with no religious background, along with Christians who are unfamiliar with the teachings of the Bible and the power inherent in the Trinity. Four common teachings derived from theosophical roots include:

1. All spiritual power is the Holy Spirit;
2. All humans have latent psychic power;
3. There is no such thing as sin and guilt;
4. We are gods.

Psychics must reduce the biblical prophets to the role of psychics and deny the deity of Jesus Christ in order to maintain their hold on their audience and their position of power. They stand in direct opposition to the truths maintained by devout Christians and seek to demote the resident power of Jesus Christ in all who align themselves with Him—to mere expressions of occult power available to all. Those powers, many believe, are latent powers of the mind that anyone can tap into.

Sin and guilt have no place in the writings of psychics because having acknowledged sin and guilt, they must acknowledge a remedy for them. Instead, they play on people's emotions, unresolved guilt and grief, and the confusion and pain resulting from tormented lifestyles steeped in sex, drugs, and materialism—and they make a decent living doing so. They offer no healing for grief, no lasting relief from their pain, and no direct God encounter.

Given the power psychics have access to—through their latent abilities and through the occult—they really have no need for one God and traditional rules and regulations associated with that God (namely, not to consult mediums or practice indiscriminate sex). Instead, they believe that they are gods with all of the power to rule themselves as they see fit, including power to manipulate the environment around them and the wills of others.

Why Not?

Why not consult psychics and mediums? After all, many reason, it's only entertainment. Mediums, spiritists, and occult practitioners are as ancient as the dust we walk on. So why is the Bible so adamantly against consulting them or getting involved with their beliefs and actions?

In Leviticus 19:31 God warns people not to turn to mediums or spirits. In Isaiah 8:19, God admonishes His people not to consult the spirits of the dead. And in Deuteronomy 18:10-12, we read, *"...who consults the dead—is detestable to the Lord...."* And when the Lord is angry, time is up, game over. Saul received his death sentence as a result of seeking out the witch of Endor (1 Sam. 28). King Ahaziah also received a death sentence for consulting an idol (2 Kings 1,2). Obviously, God does not like competition.

According to German theologian Kurt Koch, "All magic and divinatory practices are viewed in the Old Testament from the standpoint of the first commandment. The Israelite is not, in the first place, dealing with asherah images, or hobgoblins, or even with demons, but he is called with all of his heathenish practices before the bar of God. He must choose whether Yahweh is his Lord or not. He must occupy himself with the reality of God, not the existence of spirits or demons. Magic in the Old Testament is therefore not a matter of demons, but a matter which has to do with God."[5]

The Bible speaks of familiar spirits (which may be what mediums are seeing and channeling rather than the actual dead relatives), demonic spirits that are bent on deception and destruction, higher and lesser demons that have varying degrees of power, and gives Christians authority over the demons—not the other way around. God's power, ultimately, is greater.

The Old Testament speaks of the dead as messengers of God while at the same time, condemning the practice of consulting them. The witch of Endor was surprised when she conjured up not just the familiar spirit of the prophet Samuel but Samuel himself who rose up to speak to Saul. Perhaps she was surprised because she discovered that God's power was a power that could actually raise the dead while her power was limited to consulting familiar spirits—those spirits that had attached themselves to humans while they were alive and could so mimic their voice and access their "memories."

The New Testament also rejects the idea that the dead are to be sent as messengers of God. The rich man in Luke 16 asked God to send the dead to speak with his friends and relatives about the truth of salvation. He was met with the answer in verse 29: *"They have Moses and the prophets; let them listen to them."* Koch believes that the underlying message is that those who are living have access to the Word of God. That is where they can learn God's will, discover the deeper meaning to life's questions, and draw closer to the hidden secrets of the Kingdom of God.

Yet the New Testament is also full of mysteries, speaking frequently of appearances of dead people—those who may be referred to as *the cloud of witnesses* surrounding us in Hebrews 12:1 whose faith is meant to inspire us to persevere. On the mount of transfiguration Elijah and Moses come and talk with Jesus (Matthew 17:1-3), and afterward Jesus talks about his impending death and resurrection as if that was the topic of their conversation. Also, in Matthew 27:51-53 we read of those who stepped forth from their graves in the city immediately after Jesus' death:

> *At that moment, the curtain of the temple was torn in two from top to bottom. The earth shook and the rocks split. The tombs broke open and the bodies of many holy people who had died were raised to life. They came out of the tombs, and after Jesus' resurrection they went into the holy city and appeared to many people.*

The fact that they were *holy people who appeared to many people* can lead to two blatant conclusions. The first is that they were famous believers who currently form the "great cloud of witnesses" and that they may appear to people. The second is based on Old Testament Scriptures (such as the case of Saul asking the witch of Endor to summon the prophet Samuel) emphatically stating that we are not to summon or seek those who are dead. Yet Jesus, having all authority in Heaven and on earth, can release them to talk to us as *He* wills.

The Kingdom of God is manifest in healing and deliverance throughout the New Testament. Occult and demonic power is seen as creating greater psychological bondage and physical disease. Read through any of the stories of the healings and miracles of Christ and you will see the connection between the authentic power of love to set a person free and the clash of power that seeks to keep a person crippled in body and mind. God reveals through Jesus Christ that He is against demonic power yet seeks to save and heal the lost who are caught in its grip. While God hates His people to consult mediums or seek out occult power, the battle is not against us. The battle is against that which seeks to destroy us—satan. To seek out occult power and the demonic kingdom and join their beliefs is to choose against love, joy, and authentic power.

After truly tasting the marks of power that come from God—love, joy, healing, and freedom—why turn to a counterfeit that seeks to control and manipulate, offers depression and personality fragmentation? Why would a loving God allow it? To love the Lord with all of your heart and mind and soul is to turn away from opposing power and seek the face of God alone. Part of the strategy of the enemy is to call God's love controlling and satan's love freeing. Those who have not tasted of God's authentic love and power cannot possibly know the difference.

Displays of power form both kingdoms...one offers false power, a counterfeit to the true or authentic power of God. For every paranormal New Age activity in this world there is a corresponding authentic activity found in the Kingdom of God that makes satan's power look like flashy magic tricks conducted by a jealous adolescent. Until authentic power displayed through God's prophets, healers, and new creation power brokers infuses society, people will continue to turn toward the only source of power they see—occult and paranormal power displayed through television and in New Age circles.

A Word of Challenge

In our quest for the truth about who's got authentic power you will find three distinct paths open to you:

The first is to reject Christian beliefs and explore the path of the occult, consult mediums and delve into New Age teachings to determine for yourself the source of authentic power.

The second is to journey into darkness out of curiosity.

And the third, is to accept the fact that authentic power far surpasses counterfeit power and is the inheritance of every believer.

Those who follow the first path—reject Christ and seek occult power—are in grave danger and should heed the warning of Koch:

"Those involved in occult practices who do not come to a decision with regard to the question of God and of Christ stand under judgment, fall under the power of nothingness, of chaos, and end up in dependence on the powers of darkness. The converse is also true: those who accept Christ as Lord stand in the company of the Victor who came to destroy the works of the devil (1 John 3:8). [6]

Those who seek the second path—journeying into darkness out of curiosity—should heed the warning of prophet Jim Goll:

"Be careful with your curiosity. Is it the Holy Spirit who is leading you into this new experience? Is it your soulish desires or is it divine initiative? Are you being led by your passion for Jesus or is an enticing spirit leading you toward darkness by pulling on your curiosity? Many people have found themselves drawn toward the occult for the purpose of 'learning the enemy's devices,' and end up entangled in deception. The fruit is distinctly different. With an enticing spirit you are left 'beat up' and discouraged. When God is your guide on the journey of the supernatural, you are left enlightened and empowered." [7]

Those who seek the third path—accept the fact that authentic power far surpasses counterfeit power and is the inheritance of every believer—will find great challenges ahead. It is this third path that many may find most difficult because great power releases great responsibility, calls for increasing accountability, and demands an ability to hide oneself in the refuge of intimacy with Jesus as the battle rages on toward the close of this age.

Why should we care about psychics and mediums, marks of authentic power, and marks of the demonic? As we move toward the close of this age, Scripture reveals that the shifting shadows of supernatural power will increasingly clash. The darkness will grow darker. But will the light grow brighter? *You* are the light of the world. The light of Jesus Christ should be glowing ever brighter within you. As Cooke writes in the Foreword, as prophetic people we *live in the light, walk in the light, and bask in the light of all that God is to His people. [We] live with upturned faces to a God who perpetually lifts up the light of His countenance over His people. God smiles, and we look to Him and our faces are radiant.*

If we are not overwhelmed by the love of God, locked away in the heart of God's affection looking to Him with radiant faces, how can the light of the world shine through us? How can we touch the blackness and invade it? We cannot. And so we should care, very much, about not only who has the power, but who has the light shining ever brighter, reflecting His glory to a dark, dark world.

In this present and future spiritual battle where a plethora of gods, false power brokers, and demonic power sources seeks to rule and reign, we are faced with the central question the prophet Elijah called out—*If God is God, follow Him!* Making God radiant to everyone you meet is part of the plan for your life and the key strategy for defeating the dark lord operating through the occult.

ENDNOTES

1. Excerpted from the article, "Are We Creating Christian Psychics?" written by John Paul Jackson and posted on his Streams Ministries Website at www.streamsministries.com. Jackson has written many books on the prophetic ministry and focuses his ministry on dream symbolism and use of dream interpretation in prophetic evangelism.

2. Quotes and information about Kris Vallotton cited in this chapter are derived from a telephone interview. For more information about Vallotan see his church Website at www.ibethel.org.

3. Watchman Nee, *The Latent Power of the Soul.* (New York: Christian Fellowship Publications, 1972), 44, 19-20.

4. Quotes and information about Patricia King are derived from a telephone interview.

5. Dr. Kurt E. Koch, *Christian Counselling and Occultism.* (Grand Rapids, MI: Kregal Publications, 1972), 269.

6. Ibid., 273.

7. Jim and Michal Goll, *Encounters with a Supernatural God.* (Shippensburg, PA: Destiny Image Publishers, Inc., 1998), 175. The Golls are prolific authors and worldwide mentors in the prophetic gifts, intercession, and intimacy with Christ. For more information about their ministry see www.encountersnetwork.com.

   * Information about Blavatsky was derived from Francine Hornberger's book *The World's Greatest Psychics.* (New York, New York: Citadel Press, 2004), as well as the Theosophical Society's website www.theosociety.org.

   * Information about Blavatsky and Olcott was derived from the Theosophical Society's website www.theosociety.org.

   * For information about both the BSPR and ASPR societies, see the online encyclopedia Wikipedia at http://en.wikipedia.org/wiki/Society_for_Psychical_Research.

CHAPTER 4

Revelatory Power of True and False Prophets

Seers peering into the visionary shadows and prophets gazing into the stars divining the future, speaking of things to come have always titillated the public. The three most publicized "prophets" who captured the attention of popular culture in past decades claimed the capacity to peer into the future. They also all claimed to be Christians: one professed to be a Christian Sunday School teacher; and another claimed to be a prophet of God, doing the Lord's work, empowered by the same spirit that worked through Isaiah and John the Baptist. Many who watched and listened to these prophets and seers believed their power to be authentic. Over time, however, the true source of their power revealed itself.

Who is an authentic prophet? How can you tell if someone is operating from a demonic power source? What is the source of their revelation? Let's look at a few of the most famous prophets and seers in history and contemporary Christian prophets ministering today. The answers may surprise you.

Nostradamus, Cayce, and Dixon

Michel Nostradamus was a 16ᵗʰ-century French physician, the first son of a large and educated Jewish family that converted to Christianity when

Nostradamus was just a boy. During a plague that swept Europe, he gained a reputation as a gifted healer. Ironically, it was a plague that took the lives of his first wife and daughter. Devastated by the loss, he focused more on astrology and began to see his first visions. Most of his visions were written in poetic form of four-line verses in groups of 100. Many readers believe the writing was deliberately obscure to allegedly prevent persecution. Those who study his verses believe that Nostradamus predicted the rise of Hitler and World War II, the fall of New York's twin towers on September 11, 2001, and numerous world events before and between. Tabloid newspapers continue to reprint doctored translations of his poetic prophesies attributing his predictions of specific events—usually after the fact. Many find the words of Nostradamus so cryptic that they could mean almost anything. One thing all readers can agree on—the revelatory poetics are all about doom and gloom.

The visions he wrote about and historic accounts of his personal life (which I will not go into here), reflected not only the depressed state of the prophet but a budding psychosis evidenced in his fractured relationships and in the whisperings and mutterings of obscure speech.

Isaiah, the Old Testament prophet, speaks about this process of psychological disintegration in prophets who draw on the darkness of occult power rather than the authentic power of God—a power who speaks clearly to all, with revelations based on the Word of God which imparts the light of dawn.

> *When men tell you to consult mediums and spiritists, who whisper and mutter, should not a people inquire of their God? Why consult the dead on behalf of the living? To the law and to the testimony! If they do not speak according to this word they have no light of dawn. Distressed and hungry, they will roam through the land; when they are famished; they will become enraged and, looking upward, will curse their king and their God. Then they will look toward the earth and see only distress and darkness and fearful gloom, and they will be thrust into utter darkness* (Isaiah 8: 19-22).

Nicknamed "the sleeping prophet" in news articles, Edgar Cayce was born in Hopkinsville, Kentucky in 1877, a time when religious revival meetings swept through the area. Raised as a Christian with a deep interest in

64

reading the Bible, his dream as a child was to become a medical missionary. By the age of 6 he told his parents he could see visions and occasionally talk to relatives who had died. At the age of 13, he had a vision that transformed his life. In the vision, a beautiful woman appeared before him and asked what he wanted most in life. He replied that more than anything, he wanted to help others—especially sick children.

Shortly after, Cayce received every struggling schoolboy's dream: any school book he placed under him while he slept caused a photographic memory of the entire contents of the book. He discovered that he could sleep on any book, paper, or document and repeat every word no matter that the contents were—even if beyond the scope of his limited education. The gift gradually faded, though, as Cayce left school to assist his uncle on the family farm. He continued attending church, married, fathered two children, worked steadily as a photographer, and eventually became a popular Sunday school teacher who could make the Bible come alive for his listeners.

Later in life, Cayce attended a hypnotist's show and, after repeated attempts to use hypnosis to cure his long struggle with laryngitis, he discovered that while in a hypnotic state, he received information that would cure him. After he regained his speech, he recognized a newfound ability to enter a hypnotic state and give medical readings—diagnosing and giving prescriptive cures for those with a variety of illnesses. For most of his adult life, he was able to put himself into a sleep state and answer virtually any question posed to him in what became initially known as "psychic readings." Initially, the information dealt with medical problems and solutions. Eventually, he branched out into such topics as meditation, dream interpretation, and predicting future events. He drifted from his Christian faith as his "life readings" began to reflect many of the themes and terminology inherent in theosophy such as past lives, the person's potential and purpose in the present, the lost continent of Atlantis and its influence on other cultures, and higher levels of consciousness or latent power of the mind to tap into the "collective" spiritual realm.

Both his healing gift and predictions stunned and amazed the nation. He claimed to predict the beginning and end of both World War I and World

War II, the lifting of the Depression in 1933, and the coming holocaust in Europe. Even still, his other predictions are reflected in today's world events as distinct possibilities—namely, that China would become a cradle of Christianity, that Russia would be a leader in freedom and from Russia would come "the hope of the world" (a type of the antichrist), and the possibility of World War III arising in the Middle East.

In 1944, he collapsed from exhaustion and soon afterward he died.

To this day, many believe the source of his power was rooted in the authentic power of Christ. A closer look at his childhood experiences reveal otherwise. Early childhood experiences of visions, conversations with dead relatives, and a beautiful spirit woman do not present a revelation of Jesus Christ or a calling to glorify Jesus. Instead, the experiences reveal a successful demonic attempt to seduce him into a spiritual realm that was distinctly not in keeping with his Biblical upbringing, and sway him away from the religious revival of his youth. Had someone taught him in church that he was not to consult the dead; something about the difference between angels, demons, and familiar spirits; that spirits are to be tested; and that Jesus Christ is the only legal source of authentic power and vision; perhaps Cayce could have been one of the most authentic Christian prophets of the last century. The demonic had clearly intervened to make sure that Cayce would not come into the fullness of his calling as a true prophet and become their worst enemy.

Instead of releasing authentic gifts of healing—not through trances but in full conscious awareness of the presence and power of the Holy Spirit—he fell into deception and became controlled by occult power. The more Cayce gave himself over to the dissociative trance state, the more he found himself under the control of demonic spirits who sought to influence listeners into new ways of thinking rooted in Eastern religions and theosophic foundations. One of the marks of demonic power is to bind people into new ways of thinking, taking away their freedom. Rather than being remembered as a true prophet, Cayce may be remembered in history as the greatest false prophet the U.S. has seen to date...a prophet operating from demonic spirits whose mission was to shift the shadows of darkness over the light of the power of Christ and establish revelation derived from occult sources into the mainstream of the nation.

With the rise of tabloid journalism in the 1950s and '60s, Jeane Dixon became the media darling of her day. She claimed to be a prophet of God, doing the Lord's work, empowered by the same spirit that worked through Isaiah and John the Baptist. Instead, she was an amateur astrologer with a strong record of failed predictions that were blatantly ignored by media eager to entertain readers with New Year psychic predictions. Some of her predictions were accurate. The one she is most famous for is her alleged prediction of the assassination of John F. Kennedy, a prediction that some believe was actually a myth perpetuated by the media.

Her book, *A Gift of Prophecy*, published in 1952, reveals the distinctly occult source of her revelation—a large and wise snake, its eyes looking toward the East. She felt that this snake represented all wisdom and that it told her she must look to the East for revelation. She also believed that this snake would bring peace on earth, good will, and great knowledge. (Apparently, she had never read about the snake in the Garden of Eden or she may have come into a new interpretation of her vision.) Dixon's fame as a prophet and her contribution to American culture lay in popularizing astrology and firmly entrenching it into mainstream society. She also shifted the shadows of darkness over the biblical origins and gifts of true prophecy.

Many believe that those who operate in prophetic and visionary gifts in the manner of Cayce and Nostradamas are people who have a genuine prophetic gift but it is not accessed through Christ and, as a result, is not sanctified.

According to Christian prophet Paul Keith Davis, Nostradamas, Cayce, and contemporary media psychic John Edward are among those who are accessing genuine supernatural revelation. "Nostradamus had real information that could only have come from the supernatural realm; but he found a way to access outside Christ," Davis said. "In John 10, Jesus said He is the gate for the sheep, that there are those who don't come through Me, but come over the fence or climb in through some other way. He is saying that there is an access way into the spirit and He is the only legal access to that realm. Those who do come over the fence, rather than through Jesus, are robbers and thieves. They didn't submit that gift to the Lord. Anyone who doesn't come through Him as gatekeeper to the source of revelation and shepherd of the sheep is polluted."[1] Davis believes that many others like Cayce access that revelatory realm illegally and have true prophetic gifts that are totally polluted by the occult.

Davis also believes that those who begin operating out of illegally gained revelation can turn to the Lord and find themselves ministering out of authentic power. "Lots of people are born with revelatory and spiritual gifts. We have lost so many spiritual gifts to the world," he said, citing musicians like Elvis Presley and Bob Dylan in addition to contemporary psychics. "But they were never sanctified and used to feed the people of God.

"Psalms 74:14 talks about sanctifying spiritual gifts. Only when the gift is submitted to Jesus is the head, or demonic source, cut off. Once the head, or demonic source, has been cut off from the gift, it then becomes food for the people."

Contemporary Christian Prophets and Seers

There would be no counterfeit prophets if there were not also true ones. According to Scripture, true prophets are those who speak forth the mind of God under the inspiration of the Holy Spirit. In the Old Testament, God's people abdicated their desire to hear God for themselves and deferred to Moses and the prophets. In the New Testament, all believers in Jesus Christ may be indwelt with the Holy Spirit and have been given the ability to prophesy (1 Cor. 14:39). All contemporary, Holy Spirit filled believers are able to prophesy by faith and can learn the ways that God speaks as well as increase in the ability to prophesy. In a sense, this means everyone has the privilege and the obligation to hear from God for themselves.

Unfortunately, both Christians and non-Christians find themselves either apathetic about the gifts of the Holy Spirit or the role of prophets in society or worse still, they find themselves confused by the interplay of shadows on the true Light of God's power.

Rick Joyner writes in his book *The Prophetic Ministry*:

One reason there is such an increase in demonic activity in the area of supernatural experiences is to confuse the church so that she will reject the real gifts and experiences which the Lord is restoring to her. Satan knows that these are essential to the accomplishing of God's purposes in this last hour, and he can be expected to do all he can to muddy these waters. The best way for us to help clear up the mess he is making is to find the pure source of the stream. [2]

So what is the true source of the stream and who in that stream is exhibiting authentic power today?

A tall, respectable looking prophet named Paul Cain stands before the crowd reciting names or addresses of various people then gives them a prophetic word about their futures. Any skeptic would claim the "prophet" just scanned the registration list and his prodigious memory enabled him to recite what he saw. However, Cain called out one couple by their formal names, not the nicknames given on the registration list. And the address of another was not his current address—but rather a former address where events had taken place known only to the man standing, weeping as he received emotional healing and affirmation that there is a God who calls him by name and notes every place where he had ever lived.

Another prophet, Bob Jones, sits nonchalantly in his modest home. He receives angelic visitors and experiences visions from God about people who are going to cross paths and enter into ministry together; warnings about spiritual and relational attacks about to occur in a pastor's life, coming diseases that are drug resistant, future terrorist attacks, earthquakes, and out-of-season snow storms. The weather prophesies merely illustrate and give credence to the real prophetic word—usually a word of warning. He claims his hands can tell a lot about a person's destiny, the feelings in his fingers note the specific ministry calling in an individual's life.

There appear to be as many types of Christian prophets in the world today as there are personalities and purposes. Jill Austin, founder of Master Potter Ministries, is attuned to seeing angels and releases prophetic words and the presence of God to rooms full of people, encouraging a deeper level of creativity to flow through the lives of audience members—many of whom are artists and musicians.

Patricia King takes her prophetic gift and students from her prophetic evangelism schools into the streets, reaching out to drug addicts, alcoholics, street walkers, and the homeless. King and her students set up booths at fairs and sit in coffee shops offering "spiritual readings." They interpret dreams, reveal a word of destiny or affirmation, and invite them to accept Jesus into their lives in the process. Juanita Bynum leans heavily on prophetic preaching and singing to get her message to national audiences of all races.

John Paul Jackson specifically focuses his prophetic gift in the area of dream interpretation. During conferences, he either invites specific individuals to stand and receive a gentle prophetic word that unlocks the secrets of their hearts, or he invites people to talk about specific dreams and interprets them on the spot—giving the deeper meanings that reveal heart issues and spiritual callings.

Kim Clement, a South African, prophesies while he plays the keyboards. Packaging his gift this way captivates the ones he seeks to draw into deeper relationship with Christ and passion for the Kingdom of God—those enamored by Hollywood-style entertainment and today's youth.

Graham Cooke, from England, focuses his public prophetic style on releasing a deeper revelation of the nature of God into the hearts of his listeners; and acts as a prophetic church consultant for pastors around the world.

Each expresses different styles for different audiences—trying to release their gifts in every generation, in every nation of the world to unlock the destinies and specific purposes for individuals, communities, and countries. Where did they come from? And how can you tell the difference between a true and false prophet who is tapped into the source of authentic power?

Prophets have hidden in the woods trying to blend into the ecclesiastic forest or lived in inner caves, their gifting kept in the dark until called out by the Lord. These solo voices have emerged during every generation only to find themselves ultimately driven back into hiding for a variety of reasons—poor relational skills, inability to interpret their wild visions in a way a church audience can receive, criticism from churches whose biblical views excluded modern prophets, false reports about their source of power being demonic, and jealousy, among other problems. Most church movements simply did not know what to do with them, until the 1970s. And even then, many decried the prophetic movement in the modern Charismatic church as "Charismatic witchcraft." Others began treating prophets as "Christian psychics" and pushed toward them in hopes of receiving a "word" that would enable them to rise above their circumstances and change the course of either their life or their work.

While many African-American churches and Pentecostal churches have embraced the role and title of prophets, the mainstream church has been slow to accept this concept. Some authors, like John Sandford, began writing about the prophetic movement long before it was popular. Sandford's book, *The Elijah Task*, provides a foundational framework for understanding the revelatory gifts and the roles of prophets in the modern church. As a pastor and forerunner in developing counseling models that have become integrated into many churches, he was uniquely qualified to understand the psychological and spiritual origins of revelatory experiences.

With the rising influence of the Vineyard Christian Fellowship and international church renewal movement led by the late John Wimber, many denominational and Charismatic churches found themselves open to the gifts of the Spirit and experienced power encounters that they never imagined. Suddenly, the church came to value prophetic ministry and its role in increasing faith for healing and evangelism. The stage was set not only for signs and wonders, power healing and evangelism, but for those with revelatory and prophetic gifts to come out of hiding.

In the 1980s, two prophets, Paul Cain and Bob Jones, emerged from relative obscurity and were introduced to both John Wimber and Mike Bickle, pastor of the Kansas City Fellowship in Missouri. Wimber and Bickle would eventually extend their platforms of ministry to them, in effect, ushering in a new prophetic movement on a larger scale than previously received by North American churches.

During a Spiritual Warfare Conference held at the Anaheim Vineyard Christian Fellowship in February 1989, Wimber turned the microphone over to Paul Cain who espoused his beliefs about the last days ministries and a new breed of believers who would go out in power as a nameless, faceless generation of healing evangelists giving the glory to God rather than drawing it unto themselves. He then began to minister prophetically, calling out names and addresses of individuals and giving what appeared to be accurate prophetic words to many people.

Those of us listening felt a mixture of awe and shock. Those who were open to the revelatory realms stated that they experienced a dramatic increase in their ability to see visions, angels, and understand the secrets in people's hearts during conferences where Cain was present. In the months following, many with prophetic and revelatory gifts expressed with various degrees of maturity came out of the closet in their respective churches. Clearly a resurgence of interest in the revelatory and prophetic gifts, mixed with relief in the newfound freedom to talk about spiritual experiences characterized the mood of scores of believers in churches across the nation. Others varied in their opinions; many were not so enamored.

The following summer, Wimber invited Cain to speak at the Vineyard pastor's conference held in Denver, Colorado. At that time, the Vineyard movement included 240 churches, mainly in the U.S., and was at a pivotal point in its development. Many of the leaders, including Wimber, longed for direction, cohesion, and a clear vision for the future. The emerging prophets offered much for them to grasp.

Many pastors cite this conference as pivotal in releasing prophets into the limelight—a release that detoured them from their original direction but resulted in many pastors' personal renewal. Bill Jackson, Vineyard pastor and author, writes extensively about the introduction and aftermath of the prophetic movement in his book, *The Quest for the Radical Middle: A History of the Vineyard*. His personal experience reflects the sentiments of many during this time, "The aftermath of the 1989 pastor's conference was a general renewal in the movement and in individual lives. I remember coming home and pursuing God more ardently than at any other time in my life."[3]

Wimber began to share his international platform with Paul Cain and Mike Bickle on a regular basis. Additional prophets then associated with the

Kansas City Fellowship—Jim Goll, John Paul Jackson, Bob Jones, and Larry Randolph—were also given visibility opportunities. Others more loosely affiliated with the Kansas City clan, such as Wes and Stacey Campbell, Bobby Conners, Francis Frangipane, and Rick Joyner, rose to the forefront of many international platforms as well.

Eventually, a storm of controversy focusing on various individuals, disillusionment about prophesies that didn't come to pass in expected ways, confusion on the interpretation of prophetic words and visions, questionable theological foundations and agendas, and concerns regarding prophets' methodology swirled them off center stage in the Vineyard movement. Once embracing of the prophetic, Wimber sought to distance himself and return to neglected values of the Vineyard movement—namely, church planting through power evangelism and ministry to the poor.

However, the role of prophets and seers, words of knowledge and revelatory spiritual experiences such as dreams, visions, out-of-body experiences, and accessing the supernatural realm of Heaven became integrated into not only the Vineyard movement but the lives of many worldwide through these prophets. All but one of these prophets are still active in ministry today. Having suffered through the early days of controversy they have emerged stronger, wiser, more mature, and more secure in the expression of their particular prophetic and revelatory gifts. In the process, they paved the way for many to embrace and express their revelatory gifts in the church and in the world.

The renewed prophetic movement of the 1980s made many people aware—for the first time—of the existence of prophets both old and new. Prophets who had been in ministry long before the 1980s gained additional visibility and a renewed respect, including Bill Hamon, Leanne Payne, and John Sandford.

Since the 1980s, other prophets have gained visibility in North America such as Jill Austin, Shawn Boltz, Juanita Bynum, Ian Clayton, Kim Clement, Graham Cooke, Paul Keith Davis, Ana Mendez-Ferrell, Kingsley Fletcher, Neville Johnson, Patricia King, Keith Miller, Veter Nichols, Chuck Pierce, and Kris Vallotton. Today, there are many gifted prophets around the world working in their spheres of influence who have attained local, regional, national, or international recognition.

Are There Christian Psychics?

Contemporary Christian prophets are quick to point out that they are not psychics. John Sandford delineates between the two when he writes:

> "What a relief it was to learn that the Lord's servant is blind. The Lord's servant sees nothing occult. He actuates no psychological sensitivities. He sees no vision or perceptions unless the Holy Spirit reveals. This fact distinguishes the prophet from [occult-based or counterfeit] seers. A seer, like Jeane Dixon, is not a prophet. The seer sees by exertion of his own considerable psychic powers—and possibly by the assistance of demonic spirits of divination. A prophet sees only what and when the Lord opens his eyes to see. He will not peep. A seer commits the first sin of forbidden knowledge. The seer peers wherever he can and often publishes what ought to be kept secret. Not so, God's prophet."[4]

Even though Christian prophets are not psychics, many people pressure them for words of knowledge, encouragement, and affirmation as if they were. John Paul Jackson decries this trend that treat prophets as psychics:

> "For some reason, the Church has begun to view revelatory people in the same way as the world views psychics. They believe that prophetic people should have an answer anytime to anything the inquirer wants to know. They treat prophetic individuals as if they were 'Christian psychics.'

> "On several occasions, I have experienced this type of feeding frenzy. In my immaturity, I succumbed to the demand of hungry inquirers who were a part of the Body of Christ or who sat in the pew next to me. However, we do not need to be driven by this demand.

> "We as prophetic people are not in competition with occult practitioners. Nor are we to take the place of God, who longs to speak

individually to each individual through His Holy Spirit. The Lord gives all of us the assurance that if we call on Him, He will answer us in ways that will astound us (Jeremiah 33:3; Matthew 7:7).

"In the midst of the feeding frenzy for prophetic words, some revelatory-gifted people may wonder how to respond to the demand facing them. They may ask, 'If I *know* the answer to someone's question, should I feign ignorance or lie?'...

"From God's perspective, everything has a proper time or cycle (Ecclesiastes 3:1). While God may reveal to a prophetic person future events or the answer to a problem, it may not be the time to reveal it. We must walk in the Spirit of Wisdom and discern the proper times and seasons.

"God, who is all knowing, has granted to us as prophetic people a sliver of revelation. Therefore, we do not need to appear as 'prophetic know-it-alls.' We do not always have to have 'the' answer to a question or issue that is posed to us. In fact, one sign of spiritual immaturity is when we try to answer everything that is asked of us! Remember, 'Even a fool is counted wise when he holds his peace; when he shuts his lips, he is considered perceptive' (Proverbs 17:28 NKJV). Usually, a person's insecurity and need for recognition causes a person with a prophetic gift to respond prematurely and presumptively."[5]

How do we keep from turning prophets into psychics or becoming deceived by what is spoken to us by a pseudo-prophet or one who is immature in his or her gift? According to John Sandford, the answer is simple: "Do your own listening. You may, like me, not understand at the moment what He is really saying, but what He seeds into you will make sense later."[6]

Revelation Source Fueling Authentic Prophets and Seers

If we are to do our own listening, then we need to shift through the shadows of deception and determine the source of power speaking to us. There are spiritual realms and dynamics operating as surely as there are natural laws of physics. Invisible to the naked eye, most of us can only observe their effects.

Many psychics and New Age teachings refer to this revelatory realm as perhaps consisting of seven planes of existence, inhabited by angels, demons, quantum waves, spirits of the dead, and even god (his and herself).

Many prophetic ministers such as John Paul Jackson and Paul Keith Davis refer to the spiritual realm as the three heavens, identifying the biblical references and significance of the heavens as follows:

The earth's atmosphere is the first heaven.

The second heaven is the "heavenly places" referred to in Ephesians 6:12 as the abode of "spiritual forces of evil." It is a spiritual domain where satan resides—a heavenly place that is not as high as God's dwelling place (Isaiah 14:12-13). Spirit entities in this second heaven have an authority taken from Adam including deluding influences, and the ability to descend to earth's atmosphere. As a result, some accurate revelation can come from demonic sources. The key in discerning revelation or prophecy that comes from the second heaven is determining the nature and the fruit of the revelation: Does it have love, humility, and charity at its core—or does it come distinctly from the enemy to prophesy his plans?

God's abode is heaven itself—referred to as the third heaven in Second Corinthians 12:1-4 when Paul notes his experience as being caught up into the third heaven. Whether his experience took place in the body (translating him into Heaven) or out of the body (as a form of vision), he didn't know, but he described it as paradise. God, having given all authority in Heaven and on earth to Jesus Christ, can dispatch revelatory experiences and angels at will throughout all of the heavens and earth. He may also catch up believers into the third heaven and enable them to see and experience the throne room of God and walk in His Kingdom in Heaven. Those who have authentic "throne room" experiences undeniably come away with much greater revelation of who Jesus really is and what He is saying to the Church at present.[7]

In the words of the late Dr. John White, Christian psychiatrist, "When you are open to the spiritual realm you are open to the whole shoot bang." If this is true, then it becomes imperative to shift through the shadows of the second heaven's revelation so that no one walks in confusion or deceit as to the source of power behind authentic prophets and seers as opposed to those who operate from occult or demonic dynamics.

The Holy Spirit and Revelation

The pure source of the stream of prophetic revelation lies within the presence and power of the Holy Spirit. New Age psychics often refer to the revelatory spirit realm as "spirit," "holy spirit," or "spirit guide" without distinction. This leads many in their audiences to believe that because the psychic referred to the Holy Spirit, the psychic must be a Christian. Many Christian ministers also claim the Holy Spirit as their source of revelation and power but bear little of the nature of Christ when they minister.

How can you tell who has the authentic Holy Spirit-initiated revelation? Those who refer to the Holy Spirit as a power that is "just another spirit" are operating under the deceptive revelatory realm of the second heaven. Those who refer to the Holy Spirit as a person will generally respect the fact that the power wielded by the prophet is not his or her own but is, in fact, coming from the Lord God over all spirits.

R.A. Torrey discerns the subtle differences between those who minister authentically in relationship with the Holy Spirit when he writes:

> "If the Holy Spirit is a power, we'll want to get hold of it. If the Holy Spirit is a person, we'll want Him to get hold of us. If the Holy Spirit is a power, we'll want it to accomplish our will and whim. If the Holy Spirit is a divine person, we'll want to surrender more to Him in awe and wonder. If the Holy Spirit is a power, we'll be proud we have it and feel superior to those who do not. If the Holy Spirit is a Divine Person, we'll be humbled that in His great love the very Third Person of the Trinity has chosen to dwell within us."[8]

The fruit of the Holy Spirit can be clearly seen in a true prophet's ministry over time. One who knows the Holy Spirit as a Divine Person will receive and express increasingly authentic power resulting in a personality and life characterized by: love, humility, restraint, joy, vulnerability, submission, and freedom from control. They are the same marks of power defined by Richard Foster and referred to in Chapter 1.

The fruit of one who sees "holy spirit" as just another spirit source of power exhibits the marks of power that proceed from the occult and demonic realm resulting in a life characterized by: hate, pride, unbridled displays of power, depression, jealousy, inability to relate to others or allow others to speak into their lives, and a desire to control others. They will deny that Jesus Christ has come in the flesh, died for our sins, was resurrected from the dead, and is seated at the right hand of God the Father. They will not acknowledge that the Holy Spirit of God resides in our midst as comforter, counselor and one who reminds us of all Jesus says to us in His Word, releasing deeper revelation of the nature of God and the power of God. The ones operating from an occult power source may claim that it is a gift from God but they are fundamentally incapable of giving any glory to Jesus.

A prophet operating in authentic revelation and power knows the Holy Spirit as a person and may refer to the Holy Spirit as the Spirit of the Lord, the Spirit of Wisdom and Understanding, the Spirit of Counsel and Power, the Spirit of Knowledge and the Spirit of the Fear of the Lord (Isaiah 11:1-3).

The Holy Spirit is also referred to in the Bible as much more than "just another spirit." Some of the names, attributes, and capabilities of the Holy Spirit include:

- Spirit of God who hovered over the face of the waters at creation (Genesis 1:2)
- Spirit of God who caused Saul to prophecy (1 Samuel 10:10)
- Spirit of God who gave Ezekiel a vision (Ezekiel 11:5)
- Spirit who enabled Joseph and Daniel to interpret dreams and visions (Genesis 41:12-13; Daniel 1:17)
- Spirit of God who enabled Jesus to cast out demons (Matthew 12:28)
- Spirit of God who releases revelation and prophesy (Joel 2:28)
- Spirit of the Lord who releases power beyond the might of man (Zechariah 4:6; Luke 24:49; Acts 1:8; 1 Thessalonians 1:4-5)

- Spirit who releases revelatory, healing and power gifts (Hebrews 2:4; 1 Corinthians 12:1-11)

- Spirit of guidance (Romans 8:14)

- Spirit who gives rest (Isaiah 63:14)

- Spirit who gives life (John 6:63)

- Spirit who raised Jesus from the dead and can live in you (Romans 8:18)

- Spirit of the Lord who brings freedom (2 Corinthians 3:17)

- Spirit of God who is holiness (Romans 1:4)

- Spirit of the Living God who makes his Word come alive (2 Corinthians 3:3)

- Spirit of God who gives life through relationship with Him (2 Corinthians 3:1-3)

- Spirit of Adoption in the family of God who releases you from the bondage of fear (Romans 8:14-15)

- Spirit of Truth who proceeds from the Father (John 15:26)

- Spirit of Jesus who leads us to cry out to the Father (Galatians 4:6)

- Spirit of the Father who descended on Jesus at baptism and empowered him for ministry, signifying the Father's approval and authority (Luke 3:21-22)

- Spirit who inspired the Word of God (2 Peter 1:21)

- Spirit who reveals that Jesus is Lord and enables great revelation (1 Corinthians 12:3)

- Spirit who reveals the face of God (Ezekiel 39:29)

- Spirit who is the comforter (John 14:16)

- and much, much more.

Those who are filled with the Holy Spirit are endued with power from on high and have true, authentic gifts of prophesy. In Joel 2:28, the Father promises, *"I will pour out my Spirit on all people. Your sons and your daughters will prophesy…."* And in Acts 1:4, Jesus tells his disciples to wait in Jerusalem where they would receive on the day of Pentecost the gift the Father promised—the baptism of the Holy Spirit. It is a gift that cannot be bought. Yet all who operate in the gifts of the Spirit (see 1 Cor. 12) are not necessarily operating under the authority and anointing of the Holy Spirit.

The shifting shadows of revelation also involve satan masquerading as the Holy Spirit within various churches and ministries. Derek Prince, Cambridge Fellow in Ancient and Modern Philosophy and internationally known British Bible teacher who is considered one of the greatest Christian thinkers of the 20th Century, explains this phenomenon best as he urges Christians to discern the difference and recognize who is ministering in the true anointing of God:

> "In John 16:13-14 Jesus gives us a glimpse of the Holy Spirit's ministry and activity:
>
> *"However, when He, the Spirit of truth, has come, He will guide you into all truth: for He will not speak on His own authority* [literally: from Himself] *but whatever He hears He will speak: and He will tell you things to come. He will glorify Me, for He will take of what is Mine and declare it to you.* (NKJV)
>
> "So we see: the Holy Spirit does not speak from Himself; He has no message of His own. Isn't that remarkable? He only reports to us what He is hearing from the Father and the Son. Secondly, His aim is not to glorify Himself, nor to attract attention to Himself, but always He glorifies and focuses attention on Jesus. That is the second important way to identify the Holy Spirit.
>
> "Now, I want you to listen to this carefully, because it is revolutionary. Any spirit that focuses on the Holy Spirit and glorifies the Holy Spirit **is not the Holy Spirit**. It is contrary to His whole nature and purpose. Once you have grasped that, it will open your eyes to many things which are going on in the church that are otherwise difficult to understand....
>
> "When you recognize the relationship of the Holy Spirit to God the Father and God the Son, you understand that we never give orders to the Holy Spirit. When we want the Holy Spirit to do something, we address our request to the Father or to the Son.[9]

The baptism of the Holy Spirit is a gift that is not to be used to make money, or to attract people into building up the ministries and businesses of individual Christians, healers, ministers, or prophets. It is a gift that releases the intimate, personal revelation of the Father and the Son. The gifts of the Spirit are gifts of power that enable the receivers to be witnesses of Jesus Christ, to glorify Jesus as Lord and make disciples of all nations (Acts 1:8). Any other motivation for using the gifts of the Holy Spirit will expose the Christian prophet or power broker as one who operates either out of an immature, soulish source of revelation or one given over to the release of demonic spirits. Whoever treats the Holy Spirit as one responding to their command is sadly misguided. The spirit that reveals itself in power upon request may not be the Holy Spirit.

The Purpose of Prophets

Contemporary prophets issue wake-up calls to the Body of Christ, warn of future events, challenge mediocrity, reveal the shifting shadows of loyalty, and watch out for shadows of darkness that seek to invade people groups, churches, and individuals. Their purpose is not to hear the voice of God for others and issue political and spiritual edicts like Old Testament prophets. Contemporary prophets are meant to release a desire to magnify and glorify Jesus Christ, bring maturity in relationship to Him and understanding about His ways. In fact, this is their main purpose as revealed in Ephesians 4:12-13:

> *To prepare God's people for works of service, so that the body of Christ may be built up until we all reach unity in the faith and in the knowledge of the Son of God and become mature, attaining to the whole measure of the fullness of Christ.*

Since this is a never-ending task, it looks like God intended the role, or office, of the prophet to be present until the end of this age. Meanwhile, the prophetic movement continues to find ways to do what they were called to do. They are focusing less on point-and-shoot prophecies that make them look like psychics, and more on training believers to hear the voice of God for themselves through a proliferation of conferences, schools of the prophets, and supernatural ministry. And throughout the past couple of decades, the

Charismatic church has been responding to those efforts. So much so, that a fuller measure of Christ's power is being manifested through many individuals in revelation direct from God through open visions, dreams, and other ways. The efforts of contemporary prophets have been so successful that instead of calling everyone they've trained "prophets" as they attain to a higher level of faith and knowledge, they are being called simply "revelatory people." The supernatural is becoming super-Natural as individuals assume their right and their obligation to hear God for themselves.

The need for authentic, seasoned prophets to take up higher positions as watchmen and mentors will increase as the days get darker and many become enamored with false prophets and miracle workers who try to deceive even the elect...if that were possible (see Matthew 24:24).

As Christians attain to *the whole measure of the fullness of Christ*, many will be defining and redefining what this fullness will look like. Many are moving beyond the ability to prophesy, receive accurate revelation about a person's past, present, or future, or even heal the sick. They are entering into a faith level and experience level where they can not only heal the sick but work the greater works that Jesus said they would do in John 12:14. Some are going beyond—walking on water, raising the dead, and being supernaturally transported to another location or even Heaven. They are becoming not just prophets, not just healers, but new creation power brokers operating in the fullness of God's power demonstrated first through the life of Jesus Christ and now through the lives of "ordinary believers." And as ordinary believers, we all have access to the supernatural, revelatory power of God.

ENDNOTES

1. Quotes and information about Paul Keith Davis cited in this chapter are derived from a telephone interview. For more information about Davis, see his Website at www.whitedoveministries.org.

2. Rick Joyner, *The Prophetic Ministry*. (Charlotte, NC: MorningStar Publications, 1997), 78. Joyner is a prolific author. For more information, see his Website at www.eaglestar.com.

3. Bill Jackson, *The Quest for the Radical Middle—A History of the Vineyard*. (Cape Town, South Africa: Vineyard International Publishing, 1999), 210. This vastly underrated book contains not only a history of the Vineyard movement but also includes aspects of the Jesus People movement and history of the Calvary Chapel movement.

4. John Sandford, *The Elijah Task*. (Tulsa, OK: victory House, 1977), 87.

5. John Paul Jackson, "Are We Creating Christian Psychics?" See www.streamsministries.com.

6. John Sandford, *Elijah Among Us*. (Grand Rapids, MI: Chosen Books, 2002), 160. For more information about Sandford's books and Elijah House ministry see www.elijahhouse.com.

7. Based on materials from Paul Keith Davis' White Dove Ministries Website www.whitedoveministires.org and material from a telephone interview.

8. R.A. Torrey, *The Best of R.A. Torrey*. (Grand Rapids, MI: Baker, 1990), 23-24.

9. Based on a series of talks given by Derek Prince to his coworkers at Derek Prince Ministries in March 1996. The original recording of the series, "Protection from Deception", is available through Derek Prince ministries. For more information see www.derekprince.com.

   * While many books have been written about Nostradamas, this information was derived from the Nostradamas Society of America's website http://www.nostradamususa.com/html/biography.html.

   * While many books have been written documenting Cayce's life, this information was derived from the online encyclopedia Wikipedia at http://en.wikipedia.org/wiki/Edgar_Cayce

CHAPTER 5

Supernatural Power of Healers & Power Brokers

Many people believe that the next generation of Christians and occult practitioners will find themselves releasing greater measures of power—not just to prophesy or to heal the sick, but to raise the dead, walk on water, and miraculously find themselves transported from one place to another instantly. Their words will be so powerful that a curse will immediately destroy what was intended. They will be surrounded by either divine or demonic force fields of anointing. No one will know what to call them. They will likely defy all descriptions of current ministers. Christians won't be called merely prophets, healers, evangelists, pastors, teachers, or anything else. Instead, they will be Christians so radiant with the love of God that they will walk in an unprecedented anointing.

As mentioned previously, until this move of God manifests more fully in North America, people will continue to turn toward the only source of power they see—occult and paranormal power displayed through television and in New Age circles. In the meantime, the demonic realm is all too willing to imitate the techniques of Jesus, repackage it, and sell it to the masses as authentic and lasting.

Despite the shadows of deception and unbelief lingering in North America, some Christian leaders are paving the way for a greater light to shine through believers; and this dawning light will shatter the darkness. They walk in power overseas and challenge the faith of North American Christians with their stories and demonstrations of power at conferences. They have inspired a new generation of believers to engage in showdowns against demonic powers that seek to enslave the lost, armed with the Word of God and the power of the Holy Spirit. They are also challenging North American Christians as never before to recognize that God is the God of unsurpassed power.

As demonstrations of power become more commonplace in North America believers worldwide will be called out of the shifting shadows of loyalty, out of the grey areas of unbelief, to step into the increasing light of His glory. We are being called to demonstrate what Graham Cooke describes as a *boldness that comes from the heart of God. A confidence so rich it makes anything else seem like a poverty spirit.* As we step out of the shadows of doubt and deception to embrace the pure presence and power of Jesus Christ, the brilliance of His light will close out the darkness.

Christian Power Brokers

Christian power brokers and healers, those who know the power of the Cross to heal and save the lost and experience it first hand in their ministries, are too numerous to list. Many work in such remote places that their names are unknown to most of the Western world. In the past decade others have risen to the forefront of various church arenas recognized for releasing their anointing. Heidi and Roland Baker, Todd Bentley, Reinhard Bonnke, Mahesh and Bonnie Chavda, Randy Clark, Leif Hetland, Benny Hinn, David Hogan, and Henry Mandava are among those considered part of the missionary movement of healers and power brokers who carry not only the Word of God but the power of God to people throughout the world. They see prophetic and healing gifts emerging with such power that miracles abound in their ministry. They acknowledge the full meaning of Jesus' death and resurrection and embrace the Cross—a cross that includes suffering and sacrifice for the sake of releasing healing and reconciling the world to Jesus.

They know the secret to receiving more of the power of God, training others, and imparting the charismatic gifts of healing.

David Hogan, the rugged son of a Southern Baptist pastor from Louisiana, focuses his ministry among descendents of the Mayans deep in the jungles of Mexico. He launched out into ministry as a young zealous man with no ministry credentials or Bible college training. Along the way he discovered the way to increase the anointing of the power of God in his life. He, along with many other healers and power brokers, believes that the way to obtain more power is to abide in the presence of God through prayer and fasting and to remain childlike with a dependence on the Word of God. During one conference Hogan said:

> I went to the Bible and I began to find out from Genesis through Revelation, all the prayers in the Bible. I took them all and studied every one of them. I took them apart and studied them from every angle using commentaries. I wanted to know why, when then men of the Bible prayed, their words did not fall to the ground. Then I studied fasting. Because the two things that move Heaven are prayer and fasting. If you can submit your soul in prayer, and your body in fasting, God hears you.
>
> So I looked through the Bible, and this is my opinion that I am about to share with you. In my opinion the hardest thing I could come up with, the most difficult thing I could find in the Bible for God to do was once a human being is dead, to bring that person back to life again. So I decided that through the Old Covenant and the New, that there was a thread of God's power that was in both covenants. And so I decided that I was going to seek Heaven until the day came that I could walk up to a dead person and touch him and watch him get up from the dead. That is what I decided to do. I decided that it doesn't matter if I have to fast until I turn into a bone, I don't care. If I have to pray 24 hours every day, I have to have the great glory of God that it takes to change the world around me while I'm still alive. I'm going to have it. So that is what I did. I sought after that.[1]

He and his family have learned to seek the presence of the Lord consistently. And out of His presence, their hearts shape the prayers and intercessions for the people groups they seek to reach. Hogan has become a power broker—releasing the power of God to heal the sick and raise the dead, just as all believers are commanded in Matthew 10:8. Out of fasting, great power is released through Hogan and others. It is a power that captures the attention of people bound by occult influences that have gained strength for generation after generation, demonic powers that most people in North America have never seen.

Over the years Hogan has prayed for many people who died physically and saw the miraculous power of God restore them to life. He knows the power of the Cross condemns him to victory and stands in the full confidence of the Lord. He is, as Cooke wrote in the foreword, one who lives in the radiance of God, his heart captivated by His brilliance. As a result, Hogan's focus is sharp, his perceptions in high definition. He is captured by the immensity of the Father and lives in shock and awe at what He can do, experiencing first hand that He really is far above all principalities and powers. What follows is one of Hogan's stories.

So I get inside the house and there are two or three candles burning. The first thing I see is a woman in the middle of the dirt floor, holding something, rocking back and forth, and screaming. Her 9-year-old son's body is stretched out. He has been dead for four hours. I looked over by her right side, and there were two black-magic warlocks standing there. Standing next to them were two spiritist healers. Two elders from the town were also there. They hate Jesus—they are antichrists. There were many demons there.

So what should you do? Pray, believe, receive, what? Scriptures from the Old and New Testaments began to go through my mind about how different people were raised from the dead. I didn't know what to do because no one had written a book about this, except the Bible. I now know that the Bible is the only book I need for this kind of situation. I didn't know what to do. I didn't have a direct command from God. I did not have an angelic visitation, I did not have a finger write on the wall. I didn't even have a bird chirping. I had two black-magic warlocks, two spiritist healers, two antichrists, and all of them were chanting evil spells against me!

If I were a typical American, I would think *the spiritual 'airwaves' are not clean, so I can't pray. Praise the Lord.* If I were to wait for the "spiritual airwaves" to be clean, I would NEVER pray! I do "pioneer" work. No Christian has ever prayed there before. So all the "airwaves" are polluted by the demon powers. Why do you think we have the Holy Spirit? There is not a devil big enough to stop Jesus! That is the truth. Your emotions do not have any authority in the situation. Don't listen to your emotions or you will always be in trouble. What the devil says—whether it is in your mind, or spirit, or what you are seeing or feeling or tasting or touching—has no authority over what the Word of God says. What those warlocks were saying had no power over the word of God. They cannot—can NOT—stop Heaven.

I remembered what Jesus did. Scriptures began to run through my mind. I thought to myself, "Jesus probably did it right." The mother had gone back into a corner and was whimpering. I have my hand on the boy's head, and my big hands usually cover up their little heads. Then I decided to see if he was only half-dead. Maybe I could find a faint heartbeat that would be easier! I looked all over that boy for a faint heartbeat, a pulse, and there was nothing. So I said, "He must be all the way dead."

So I began praying for him. I prayed in English. That didn't work. I prayed in Spanish. Uh-oh, that didn't work. I prayed in Indian. Uh-oh, that didn't work. I prayed in "tongues." Uh-oh, that didn't work. That was all of the languages that I knew. What should I do? I told you already, I can't give the credit to anything but the name of Jesus. I can feel God's Spirit on me now and I feel like He is carrying me away. I think I was so nervous that I was praying a few words in one language and then in another. But in every language, the name of Jesus was there, and that is what is important. "How long?" I have no idea. I know that I began to sweat a lot, but it was a hot night, around 38 degrees Celsius [100.4 Fahrenheit] at 11 o'clock at night. I was praying and sweating and holding onto the little boy's arm. He was stiff and sticky, and had lost all of his color. He was whiter than I am and usually they are almost black.

Suddenly, while I was praying—the little boy was wearing a t-shirt—the father and I saw the t-shirt bounce. I looked at the father and his eyes were as big as mine, because he saw it also. But the devils are still standing there chanting. They are still angry and cursing God and me and everyone else. For some reason, that didn't bother the Holy Spirit. What do you think of that? The Holy Spirit came into the room, thumped the heart of that little boy and made it work again. In a few minutes, his little arm became limp. And then—listen—the color came back into him. He became warm again. WOW! Some of you may be thinking "David, you should calm down!" but you are wrong! Maybe tomorrow, because today is the day of salvation, just like when Jesus was raised from the dead. Today is the day of power and resurrection. Today is the day of glory! Today is the day of visitation.

I don't know why God came into the room and through me, or however He did it, to heal that boy. I don't feel qualified or adequate. I don't feel like I have enough Bible knowledge. But that doesn't seem to bother the Holy Spirit if I feel that way, as long as I call on the name of Jesus in faith. As long as I believe that "All things whatever you ask in prayer, believing, you shall receive." That is what I believe. That is what the Bible says. Listen to me. I didn't know what to do next, because his eyes opened and he looked at me. Almost all of the children are afraid of me because I am so big to them. But this little boy was in perfect peace. I picked him up—this is wonderful—this little boy who is alive, who was dead for a little over four and a half hours.

Heidi and Roland Baker focus their ministry in Mozambique, Africa, among a Muslim population that has suffered through droughts, wars, and disease for generations. The Bakers are power brokers who know that the power of the Cross condemns them to victory and to walk in the confidence of the Lord. They have seen blind eyes opened, the deaf suddenly hear, and the dead raised to life as routine events in their ministry and through the ministry of pastors they train throughout the world.

They, too, have discovered that the secret to releasing the power of God is to dwell in the presence of God through prayer and fasting. They spend countless hours soaking in the love of God and interceding for those to whom they minister. Their intimacy with God provokes confidence that releases faith to stand in God's presence and see Him as big as He is. They live in a place rife with the external evidence of demonic control—war, disease, famine, and corruption. Yet their internal dwelling is what Cooke calls the place of *refuge, a fortress, a secret place of worship and communion. They access a place of blinding, coruscating light. From that place they embark on their mission, to magnify the Lord in the world of men.*

Along the way, fasting has become a way of life for them as well. The explosive growth of their ministry is due to the miraculous power that God has released through them in the past decade. The Gospel is advancing whole villages at a time as the Holy Spirit's power is poured out.

How does this happen? Here is one example from the Bakers.

Felito Utuie, a 22-year-old evangelist we have nurtured in the Lord, was trying to get a Muslim chief of a village to grant permission for an outreach. The chief repeatedly refused. Felito told him that Jesus would heal the sick. Finally, the chief asked, "If you come, will I see that happen?" "Yes!" Felito answered simply. So the chief agreed to a meeting in his village.

On the night of the outreach, the meeting began with a very quiet, open atmosphere, unlike some gatherings we have where at first we face loud demonic disruptions. Felito preached the pure, simple Gospel and asked, "Who recognizes their need of a Savior?" Voices cried out in the dark, "I want forgiveness! I want forgiveness!" A great noise arose as the people pleaded for salvation and streamed forward to pray. Then Felito announced that he and his team would pray for the sick. Healings occurred one after another. A mother brought her 8-year-old boy who was deaf, and he was instantly healed. Felito asked the chief, "Do you see?" Immediately the chief asked for the microphone and told his own people, "This is real! No man can do this! Only God can do this! Bring more of the sick! Bring all the sick!"

One man brought his little 7-year-old daughter who was totally blind. She received prayer, and her father urgently asked her, "Do you see?" And then tears began streaming down his face as his daughter looked and saw his face for the first time in her life! And the healings continued that night....

All this last year our outreaches have been frequently bearing this kind of fruit. We don't preach long or get complicated. The people respond in simple faith, and as soon as they see Jesus is real and will touch them miraculously, they want Him! They want salvation, they want a church, they want a pastor, now! Their chiefs beg us, "Don't leave us! You can't leave us like this! We've never seen miracles like this! You have to come back and teach us!"

Heidi especially has received a special anointing for the deaf, blind, and lame, and sees them healed at nearly every outreach. Once she prayed late at night for a crippled and blind man who was not healed right away. But she told the village to send a runner to tell her as soon as he was healed. The following day she was with a Muslim friend and leading businessman in town when a runner ran breathlessly up to the window of the car they were in. "He is healed! He can walk and see!" The runner had just run seven hours to tell her.... "In tears and awe, our Muslim friend cried, "Pray for me! Pray for me now!"[2]

Who Can Move in Power?

As forerunners like the Bakers and David Hogan speak of their stories, many people are being inspired to move out in the presence and power of

God. Middle-aged couples are selling their homes and moving to the mission field while an army of young power brokers is being raised up through schools of supernatural ministry launched through various pastors and ministries around the world. Through the efforts of Randy Clark and others, a new missionary movement of power brokers is being launched that is dependant not on mission boards and programs to send them, but on the presence and power of the Holy Spirit leading them into various arenas in the world and in the workplace.

Randy Clark, a former Vineyard movement[see inserted footnote about the Vineyard] pastor turned revivalist after God used him to spark worldwide revival beginning in Toronto, has launched a series of healing schools across the nation. Clark's motive for launching the healing schools is to clear away the debris of wrong theology and to equip the saints to heal. "I believe that we are going to see another healing revival so I wanted to establish a school where there could be a solid biblical basis for both the models and the theology behind healing and power evangelism. People like the models I learned in the Vineyard and the balance so I do expect that there will be a multiplication of healing in churches, communities, and nations as a result of our healing schools."[3]

Through his healing schools, conferences, and international ministry trips, everyday ordinary believers are caught up in a new dimension of supernatural healing and power. Many individuals receive not only a biblical understanding about the gift of healing, they also receive an impartation of faith and power to lay hands on the sick and heal them. Ordinary believers become extraordinarily transformed after experiencing ministry trips with Clark's Global Awakening ministry. Clark, in fact, has been used to impart greater gifts of healing to Heidi and Roland Baker and Leif Hetland, a Norwegian pastor, during critical points in their ministries.

According to Clark, not everyone can lay hands on another for impartation of healing gifts. "This [impartation ability] is a gift, and within Christianity it is done under the anointing of the Holy Spirit and accompanied often with a prophetic word. This cannot even be done by the person when he/she wants, but has to be initiated by the Holy Spirit." And during those

Holy Spirit-initiated moments, Clark was moved to prophesy a great release of anointing and impart, through the laying on his hands, an ability to heal beyond what the recipients had ever experienced before.

As an unassuming young senior pastor of a small Baptist church in Sandnas, Norway, Lief Hetland had no idea that he would one day find himself leading hundreds of thousands of Muslims to Christ during the most tense decades of Mid-East and Western relations. Although he had some experience with global mission work—primarily in Africa and Eastern Europe—he considered it more of an accident when miracles happened.

Struggling to understand the role of both Word and Spirit in evangelism while burning out in ministry, he heard that Randy Clark was coming to Norway and decided to attend the meeting. To his surprise, Clark prophesied over him and released an impartation for increased miracles and anointing that would become evident within the coming years. However, immediately after the prophetic word, Hetland was in a serious car accident that left him flat on his back for a year. During recovery God revealed His heart for Muslims and a strategy for Hetland to minister in Muslim nations.

"I had to see that Muslims were a promise that can only be received, not a problem. Second, to not live by fear but live by love. Love is a more powerful language, the language that blind eyes will see and deaf ears will hear. The people will not know how much you know until they know how much you care," Hetland explained.[4]

"After this impartation I had different glasses on and saw very clearly what was the Father's heart for unreached people and that miracles were key tools to bring the Gospel. To proclaim the Gospel I had to have a demonstration of the Gospel in a lot of places," Hetland continued. It was while ministering in Pakistan that he noticed God sovereignly healing individuals who were unknown to Lief but well known in their community. The demonstrations of God's power turned many hearts toward Jesus and the barrels of many guns away from Leif.

Clark and other healers and power brokers believe that everyone can heal the sick. In fact, the Lord specifically commands and commissions us to pray for the sick, cast out demons, cleanse the lepers, and raise the dead as part of the apostolic commission of the New Testament.

According to Clark, "We don't expect the liberals who deny the supernatural dimension of life to pray for the sick. Neither do we expect the Cessationists who believe that it's no longer possible to pray with faith to heal the sick. But we do expect those Charismatics and Pentecostals and third-wave evangelicals who believe praying for the sick is still for today to pray for them. Because if not you—who? Who is God going to use? More people will find God's power increasing in the Church when they are stepping out and releasing God's power."

In the meanwhile, the power of the Holy Spirit to heal has been continuously mocked and ignored by both professing Christians and unbelievers throughout the world. Instead, many gravitate toward the counterfeit healing techniques of demonic power brokers and healers.

Shifting Shadows in the Healing Movement

Throughout the centuries, people have gravitated toward faith healers seeking cures for physical and emotional problems that lie beyond the hope of medical science. They gathered around Jesus seeking a healing touch. In our world today, individuals gather around anyone who promises healing—witch doctors, physicians, New Age practitioners, and Christian healers. If one technique fails, another promises hope. New Age and Christian healing centers abound. We call them medical clinics and hospitals, naturopathic offices and health food stores, and healing prayer rooms. People move easily from one to the next. In North America, Christians move nonchalantly between Eastern and Western medical practices, buy up the latest neutraceutical that promises health or anti-ageing properties and head off to a Christian healing room only as a last resort. In Brazil, many move between the Catholic rite for healing to Macumba witchcraft, and finally head off to hear a healing evangelist in hopes of a cure. In other countries residents seek out witch doctors between visits to Western physicians—if they can find a physician.

According to both New Age and Christian healers, we will see an increased interest in healing centers and healing evangelists in the future. As medical science fails to find cures for the common cold, AIDS, new flu strains, and a host of diseases and afflictions, people will become more desperate to find someone, anyone, who can offer them hope and relief from suffering.

Psychic Sylvia Brown also believes that a healing revival will take place in the near future. Her version includes huge healing centers located in power spots around the world like Sedona, Arizona, and structured so that crystal pyramid energy can flow down through the roof to individuals below. Inside the building, New Age healers will release the wonders of Reiki, Johrei, and Qi Gong. Herbalists, acupuncturists, and massage therapists will ply their trades. Some healers will simply lay hands on people and watch as their bodies sway into a wave-like motion or go suddenly limp as if they are losing consciousness for a split second. While the recipients of healing appear to manifest in much the same away as those receiving healing from Christians, the source of healing power is distinctly demonic. Some people report that the demonic residue also impacts the recipients for years afterwards.

Deepak Chopra's quasi-Eastern healing center appeals to the wealthy. Located in Carlsbad, California, an affluent beach community in the San Diego area, clients walk into his center devoid of life, materialism having robbed them of any true joy and peace. They leave more radiant, having received, if not a healing touch, at least some hope, compassion, and a temporary shot of love. He appeals to their love-starved souls and offers help through a paid therapeutic practitioner.

Other healing spas throughout the country incorporate a variety of healing techniques and philosophies, appealing to the masses with more limited funds. Consumers flock to these centers in hopes of finding a cure for their emotional and physical afflictions.

Consumers often look more to spas and retreats than individual clinics and yet, only a few Christian healing centers are open in North America for those who can afford to pay for in-patient care and intensive treatment without medical insurance assistance. The Seventh Day Adventists have been on the forefront of offering holistic healing—opening healing centers, hospitals, and retreats focused on biblical principles of health through nutrition and prayer and espousing vegetarianism. Other Christian centers and hospices offer respite for cancer patients and assist them in bringing closure to their lives. Most do not offer healing prayer for either emotional or physical healing. Only recently Charismatic believers are planning to open healing centers focused on acute emotional and medical needs: centers that will address nutrition, inner healing, healing prayer, and spiritual growth alongside medical and chiropractic techniques.

Meanwhile, Randy Clark believes another form of healing revival is underway and growing in power—a healing revival for the masses. This revival includes many leaders who are developing their healing gifts and faith and taking it to the streets of developing countries and even the streets of U.S. cities.

But all that glitters is not gold. As Christians release God's authentic healing power, a counterfeit movement continues to morph out of Eastern religions combining theosophy, quasi-scientific, and spiritual principals. It seeks to capture a whole post-modern population struggling with the illnesses of life, those who appear to be irreligious yet long for some spiritual connection with the universe.

Counterfeit Laying On of Hands

Just as Christians receive an impartation and anointing to lay hands on individuals and heal the sick, counterfeit power and techniques cloak the world in shadows today. The dark lord wants to deceive Christians, releasing doubt as to the origins of God's authentic power. The occult powers want to create confusion and release doubts that cause Christians to ask: if unbelievers can heal the sick through the laying on of hands, then what is the power of Jesus Christ all about? Should Christians even reach out and touch someone or is it all New Age and demonic?

Parallel dimensions of healing flow through the world. One is distinctly Christ-centered, dependent on the gifts of the Holy Spirit to discern the emotional or demonic origins of ill health and releasing healing through prayer. The other ensnares unbelievers in the shadows that look like God's power at work but contain language and spiritual sources of healing that are distinctly not from God.

The newer techniques emerging on the New Age market closely parallel Christian healing techniques and include Matrix Energetics and The Reconnection. They both spring off from Reiki healing but the founders claim their techniques are based on the laws and expression of subtle energy physics, such as quantum physics and superstring theory. Practitioners claim that they feel intense energy in their hands or heat in their hands as they heal. Their practice of healing through Matrix Energetics or Eric Pearl's Reconnection technique, looks eerily similar to the Charismatic Christian practice of "laying on of hands" for healing. The results, too, look as if people are feeling overwhelmed by God's presence and that the "anointing" to heal others is transferable...for a few thousand dollars.

Those who are touched by a Matrix Energetics practitioner often feel a wave-like motion when Matrix Energetics is applied. The body seems to instantly drop in a completely relaxed wave. The participants are taught specific methods of using a powerful, focused intent, combined with application of a light touch method for identifying the parts of the body where the Matrix Energetics "wave" will yield optimum results. Practitioners believe that the wave is a result of the unconsciousness and the biological physical fields interacting. Videos of the healers in action look amazingly like Christians who lay their hands on a person and see the power of God wash over them, causing many to drop to the floor.

Eric Pearl, a chiropractor based in Hollywood, developed The Reconnection Seminar after his patients reported that they felt his hands on them—even though he hadn't physically touched them. During the first few of months operating in this newfound power, Pearl's palms blistered and bled. According to The Reconnection Website, patients reported seeing angels and receiving miraculous healings from cancers, AIDS-related diseases, cerebral palsy, Chronic Fatigue Syndrome, birth disfigurements, and other afflictions. The healings occurred when Pearl simply held his hands near them.[5]

Glancing at his seminar brochure it's easy to misconstrue the brochure as an advertisement for the latest Christian conference. A picture of Michelangelo's finger of God reaching out to touch man splashes across the page. The "Reconnection" is easily misread as "The Resurrection" and the laying on of hands for healing is acknowledged without using overt spiritual language. Spirituality is deliberately removed from bold print to lure readers into a more scientific-sounding approach to healing. Yet it is interesting to note that New Age entities blatantly mimic terminology, techniques, and manifestations of the Holy Spirit.

But a closer look at the brochure reveals the true spiritual source of healing. They call this source "God," "love," or "universe." Jesus is nowhere to be found. However, they promise that as one progresses through seminar levels they will establish a powerful connection with the source of healing—a demonic source that counterfeits what Christ has already released through the gifts of the Holy Spirit.

Through three progressive seminars, participants in The Reconnection learn how to access "frequencies of healing" that come to the hands as a "continuum of energy, light, and information." As they practice laying hands on each other for healing, the practioner-in-training will notice "involuntary movements of the face, head, and body in those they work with as you guide them into healing realms beyond those previously accessible."

The second level seminar promises that participants will "permanently establish a powerful connection with the source of these healings." To progress to the next level trainees must schedule an appointment with a Level III practitioner for $333—a fee designed to "maintain the integrity of the 333 vibration with which the Reconnection was and is brought in." The Reconnection is performed on two separate days.

The final level is designed to reconnect individuals with what they call the larger universe of axiatonal lines—grid lines that encircle the planet and cross at acknowledged power places such as Machu Picchu and Sedona. The founders believe that these lines are part of a timeless network of intelligence, a parallel-dimensional system that draws the basic energy for the renewal functions of the human body.

According to the brochure, "This level teaches how to bring in and activate these new lines, allowing for the exchange, beyond energy, of light and information, the reconnection of DNA 'strands' and the reintegration of 'strings' (simultaneously occurring parallel planes of existence)."

How will the world respond to these shadows of counterfeit supernatural power? The audience these New Age healers seek include disenfranchised Christians and those who have not gravitated toward any brand of spirituality in the past...a group that is neither Christian nor New Age in its bent, but rather enamored with quasi-rationalistic and sci-fi power. As a result of gravitating toward these counterfeit healing techniques, they will be referring to the Holy Spirit as "reconnection power" rather than a member of the Trinity. In short, they are being inoculated against the truth and heeding the doctrines of demons that contain a measure of truth. They will be slow to discern the source behind the "healing power" they practice. Indeed, it may take a huge power encounter to cause the source of their power to rear its ugly head.

But who is up to the task of unmasking such subtle evil, much less the more overt evil evidenced on overseas mission fields?

Hot Spots and International Healing Rooms

Psychic Sylvia Brown may be correct in her prophetic view of healing centers popping up around the world. But they look far different from what she imagined. Various "hot spots" are emerging across the U.S. where individual churches are gaining reputations for becoming healing centers. Places like Bethel Church in Redding, California, have sought the presence and power of God to fill the atmosphere of their church and community in hopes that it will become a "cancer free zone." Many who have sought healing for various conditions, including terminal cancer, have received healing while attending church services, conferences, or just spending time in their prayer house located on the church property. Grace Center in Nashville, Tennessee; New Life Church in Las Vegas; and both Life Center and Christ Community Church in Harrisburg, Pennsylvania, are finding that the presence of God is resident to heal.

In addition to individual churches becoming healing centers, the success of the International Healing Rooms movement is also fueling the current focus on healing evangelism. Many people are gravitating toward a worldwide ministry, which originated in Spokane, Washington, for more personal, intensive prayer—and the results are frequently amazing.

The International Association of Healing Rooms (IAHR), led by Director Cal Pierce, has sparked a healing movement that is sweeping across the nation, focusing on training lay people to release the presence and power of God to heal. The healing rooms movement encourages local churches to band together to open a healing room where trained volunteers spend hours praying for those in need.

"In the past we've relied on healing evangelists to come into the community, do a crusade, and leave, taking the anointing with them," Pierce said. "Now the healing anointing is coming into the Church. Our commission is to see cities transformed. The work of the healing rooms is to heal the body (the Church) so the body can evangelize the city by releasing the healing presence of God."[6]

In 1996, Pierce experienced a dramatic encounter with God, and three years later found himself reopening the healing rooms of Spokane that were initially established by healing evangelist John G. Lake 80 years prior.

"We started with eight people praying for the sick on the very location that John G. Lake had owned and people came from all over," said Pierce about Lake, a healing revivalist active in the early 1900s with a worldwide ministry launched out of Spokane, Washington.

At present, 140 volunteers from a variety of churches—Baptist, Presbyterian, Charismatic and Pentecostal—pray for upward of 1,000 people a month who flock to the IAHR in need of physical and emotional healing. The ministry now owns a 15,000-square-foot building, operated by a staff of 35, that serves as a world training facility, teaching individuals how to pray for the sick as well as raising up regional directors to oversee other healing rooms.

Volunteer candidates are monitored to ensure they have the appropriate skills for the healing ministry. In addition, they train in established healing rooms before launching their own center.

As a result of Pierce's ministry, 300 additional healing rooms affiliated with his organization are now located in 20 nations, and countless others have opened on their own or through local churches in the United States. Healing rooms typically have set hours for prayer and do not charge for their services.

Most of the people who come to the healing rooms suffer from illnesses that are not visible to the prayer team, such as cancer, arthritis, and diabetes. Pierce said, "Some are healed instantly, others return frequently until they have received a measure of healing or a complete healing. Because healing can be so progressive, we never make the assumption that they were not healed after being prayed for."

Results are often noted days, weeks, or months after receiving prayer when a person notices that their symptoms have abated or a physician documents the healing. Many healing rooms have physicians taking note and in some instances verifying the healings. In Seattle's Harborview Hospital physicians were amazed to see symptoms quickly abate in terminally ill people and other patients completely healed after a hospital social worker prayed for them. As a result of her success, hospital administrators gave her space and permission to open a healing room in the hospital.

"Some people come in expecting a miracle and they take hold of it right away," Pierce said. "But healing itself is a process."

He told the story of one woman who was HIV-positive for 20 years and for whom they prayed for more than five months. During that time, Pierce said that as the prayer and Word was built up in her, the levels by which HIV is measured dropped to undetectable levels.

"Not only did Jesus heal her body, she now has a ministry here," he said. "Had she come in and received an instant healing she would have missed her destiny to minister to those who are on the street."

Skeptics of Divine Healing

Despite the interest and overwhelming need for divine healing, many evangelicals are skeptical of faith healers and movements. Pastor and author Joe McIntyre of Seattle, Washington, has researched the topic for years and discovered that the late 1880s divine healing movement was actually spread by such evangelical leaders such as Andrew Murry, A.D. Simpson (founder of Christian Missionary Alliance), and A.J. Gordon, respected Baptist leader in Boston who wrote a book on healing.

The current Charismatic Christian healing movement was fueled by the ministries of John G. Lake and E.W. Kenyon during the early 1900s. Lake solidified his reputation as a healing evangelist during several years in Africa when thousands who attended his meetings received miraculous healings. After Lake left Africa and settled in the Spokane, WA area, he opened the first of many healing centers. Between 1913 and 1920, more than 100,000 people were estimated to be healed at the famous "healing rooms" that were located in downtown Spokane's old Rookery Building.

During the 1920s, Kenyon, a Free Will Baptist preacher, gained a reputation as a healer for miraculous healings that reportedly accompanied his preaching. His focus on understanding the Father-heart of God, who we are in Christ, and the authority and privileges of the believer still echo through many current ministries.

According to McIntyre, both Lake and Kenyon believed in Dominion theology, which is also the basis of the current Healing Rooms ministry.

"It is an aggressive approach that believes we are supposed to demonstrate the kingdom of God with power, not just words," McIntyre explained. "Much of the church passively waits on God's sovereignty rather than taking the kingdom. God wants to keep his promises, but we need to develop our faith to receive and aggressively take them."[7]

McIntyre also believes that the criticism against faith healing stems from a Greek and rational worldview of Scripture. "The reason we reject healing and Christ's work is because our view of Scripture is not Hebrew, it's Greek," McIntyre said. "Cessationism, the idea that God doesn't do miracles today, is a Greek idea. In the Hebrew worldview all of life is holy and important and to be lived with a thankful heart. As we return to the Hebrew worldview, the scripture that says He bore our sickness and pains (Isaiah 53) is an argument for Christ's atonement providing healing as well as forgiveness."

Cal Pierce, a fellow practitioner, agrees. "Dispensationalist teaching leads us to believe we hope they are healed but you don't pray for the lost and hope they're saved," he said. "Why can we impart salvation by faith but not for healing? They are not separate issues; they come from the same place—the word of truth."

Regardless of criticisms about the modern faith movement, McIntyre said he believes that the greatest sin in the body of Christ is unbelief. "We haven't believed the Gospel," he said. "A critic of the faith movement, Gordon Fee, said that he was against the faith movement but if he were to measure the level of faith existing in the evangelical church it would be a minus five. To me that says we may not like everything coming out of the faith and healing movement, but at least they're seeking God to have more faith."

Also fueling the criticisms over healing are controversial stories about charlatans—Christians who launch themselves into a ministry of healing while devoid of true anointing or solid character. As a result, they are often exposed when someone draws the curtain back and instead of finding Jesus, see a mere man, blowing his own horn and stage managing a charlatan's show. The marks of power that come from God—love, humility, restraint, joy, vulnerability, submission, and freedom from control—have given way to greed and narcissistic desires to be seen and worshiped.

According to Bill Johnson, author and senior pastor of Bethel Church, who has an international teaching and healing ministry, too many people are embarrassed over the abuses of power rather than the lack of power moving through their own lives to build the Kingdom of God. He believes that critics are often justifying their own lack of pursuing the gifts of the Spirit and obeying Jesus' command to heal the sick, raise the dead, and make disciples of all nations in the process of speaking forth the Word of God with accompanying signs of the power of God.

Johnson writes in his book, *When Heaven Invades Earth*: "When I see others who have pursued great things in God but have failed, I get motivated to pick up where they left off. The abuses of one person never justify the neglect of another. Many of those who are embarrassed over the abuses of power, and the subsequent blemishes on the Church, are seldom offended over the absence of signs and wonders. The eyes of the critics quickly move to the ones who tried and failed, overlooking the countless millions who confess salvation in Jesus, but never pursue the gifts as commanded. But the eyes of Jesus quickly look to see if there is faith on the earth—*When I return will I find faith on the earth?* For every charlatan there are a thousand good citizens who accomplish little or nothing for the Kingdom."[8]

Shifting Shadows of Complacency

As we move into the close of this age and a coming showdown between counterfeit power brokers and God's power brokers on a mass scale, complacency endangers the outcome for many. Demonstrations of God's authentic power can only come from a heart that is wholly surrendered to Him, confident in His compassion and ability to heal.

Complacency is an erosion of faith, the remnants of a bonfire of passion that dwindled to mere embers of desire. It is a controlled, passionless relationship with the Father of Life. Complacency is the ultimate victory of satan's scheme against all Christians. It means that you have shifted your gaze off of the Lord and pulled the shadows of past doubt and despair, woundings and failures, like a blanket over your head. Rather than taking refuge in the presence of the King, you have colluded with the enemy's desire to draw you into his realm of passion—that of robbing you of the fullness of life, the abundant life the Father of Life has promised.

Elijah's task was to call the people of God out of their complacency. That was part of the reason for the showdown at Mt. Carmel. And as soon as they stepped out of that place of colluding with the dark powers of their age, they turned and fought against the darkness. The prophets of Baal lay slain on the battlefield at the hands of God's people. The principalities and powers of this age have already been overcome by the death and resurrection of Jesus Christ. We are condemned to victory. And each one has a specific invitation to join in the work of the Father, to inherit the Kingdom, and to slay the powers of darkness around us. But first, we must step out of the shifting shadows of complacency and back toward the bonfire of God's love. Authentic marks of the power of God are rooted in His love. All other counterfeit power pales in comparison.

The Price of Power

If the power of the Cross condemns us to victory, as Cooke says, then we must become believers who have a passionate desire to win. No matter where individuals carry the presence and power of God, they all have one thing in common—the firsthand knowledge that there is a price to pay for the anointing to heal the sick, raise the dead, and perform miracles. A passionate desire to win will overcome the temptation to succumb to discouragement and temper the heartache involved with sharing in the suffering of Christ that comes with becoming a power broker in the Kingdom of God. A passionate love for Jesus and knowledge of His passionate love also sustains those who are paying the price of power.

According to Randy Clark:

> If you are to prepare for an increase in power, you must understand that walking in the power of the Holy Spirit involves suffering and a continual humbling process. Not everyone you pray for will be healed. Your heart will ache over those who are desperate for a touch from God and don't receive the miracle they seek.

> One night, I watched John Wimber pray for people gathered together in a Methodist church. Miraculously, almost everybody was healed when he prayed for them. The power of God was definitely present to heal. The next night, however, no one was healed.

> I talked to John about it after the abysmal meeting ended and said, "I don't understand it."

> He replied, "You don't get it do you? I don't have any more sin in my life than I did last night. I don't have any less faith tonight than I did last night. Last night I came here, put my fat hand out and said, 'Come Holy Spirit.' I just blessed what I saw God do. Last night when everyone got healed I didn't go to bed thinking I'd done anything great or I was some great man of God. And tonight I'm not going to be feeling like I am a great failure either. It wasn't me either time. And tomorrow I'm going to get up and do it again."

That short conversation with John encouraged me to step into the healing ministry. For the first time I saw the humanity and the brokenness behind the man who wielded such power. When I realized that the power was a result of the anointing and not John, I said in my heart I can do this. I can embrace this ministry because I learned his secret: Just show up, just put yourself in the place of ministry. Don't take yourself too seriously. Learn how to see what the Father is doing and bless it.

In Luke 5:17 the Spirit of the Lord was present to heal. The implication is that it wasn't always that way. But it is extremely difficult when you're in that place where the miracles aren't coming to the worst cases. I was ministering in Brazil recently and grieved after I prayed for a little boy with a severe case of Cerebral Palsy. The boy wasn't healed. I also prayed for a girl who was deaf in both ears. Despite the fact that I've seen a lot of deaf people healed, she wasn't healed. That night I didn't go to bed thinking I was a great failure and tomorrow, I am going to get up and do it again.

Despite heart-wrenching nights of ministry like that one, I take encouragement in the fact that there are divine appointments. Recognizing the divine appointments helps me separate from the sense of obligation that I have to pray for every sick person that I see. Jesus didn't pray for every person he saw. Suffering is lessened by understanding how to obey the spirit, recognizing who you are supposed to pray for, and not feeling guilty because you passed somebody else up.

Entering into the powerful ministry of Jesus is not all suffering. There is an excitement about it as you look to the divine appointments where you know that you are to pray for someone and that they will be healed or saved. You never know when God is going to show up and release His power. You could be at work, at play, or at home when God gives you a prophecy or a word of knowledge for healing. As you act on that prompting of the Holy Spirit, all Heaven breaks loose. No sweat. Our ministry is to be yoked to Jesus. His burden is light. When we feel like it's no longer light or easy, we're pulling too much.

Heidi and Roland Baker articulate the price they pay as they come against the demonic strongholds—a price that includes theft of ministry resources, sickness, malicious lies, and political backlash. They, along with David Hogan, have faced guns and violence. In fact, Hogan has been shot and beaten in his pursuit of the Kingdom, and even left for dead. Not one New Creation Power Broker on the mission field today leads an easy life coasting along in a bullet-proof bubble of the Holy Spirit, untouched by human suffering and demonic backlash.

The Bakers share their mission field perspective:

> Some who hear us in conferences may come away with the impression that we lead a charmed, tribulation-free life of endless miracles! We do prefer to give Jesus and His glorious power most of the attention in our ministry, but it many encourage you to know that, like Paul, we are jars of clay who glory also in our weakness. When we are weak, then we are strong (2 Cor. 12:10). We do encounter fierce, demonic opposition, and its intensity is almost incomprehensible. This Mozambican province where we live has been a pagan, occultic stronghold for centuries, and the evil we encounter shocks us over and over. Our time, energy, funds, and resources are viciously attacked and drained as the devil aims to turn our hearts away from this great revival in which God has graciously placed us.
>
> Together with Paul, we understand that these things happen that we might not rely on ourselves but on God, who raises the dead (2 Cor. 1:9). We resist the devil by overcoming evil with good, and by resting in Him with all the more faith and childlike joy. We cannot lose while secure in His heart. We have no need to shield ourselves, but we entrust our souls to a faithful Creator in doing what is right (1 Peter 4:19). The God who has raised at least 53 people

from the dead among our churches in Africa will also renew and refresh us with His incomparable power. He will not fail us; we are His workmanship!

In North America, few Christians are willing to take to the streets and speak the truth. Even fewer have developed their relationship with Christ far enough to rise to a level of faith and anointing that will shake others out of the shadows of deception. We can no longer afford to be complacent as the shadows of the end of the age close in around us. We must step out of the shadows of complacency and stand in the brilliance of God's amazing love. And having stood soaking in His light, understanding His ways, we realize that the power of the Cross condemns us to victory in whatever action He calls us into, in whatever sphere of influence He gives us.

ENDNOTES

1. The information and stories cited in this chapter are based on a transcript of David Hogan's message given in Spokane, Washington, and a Website at www.fuegodedeios.com.

2. All quotes in this chapter are excerpted from newsletters posted on Heidi and Roland Baker's Iris Ministries Website at www.irismin.org.

3. Quotes and information about Randy Clark cited in this chapter are based on a personal interview. For more information see www.globalawakening.com.

4. Quotes and information about Leif Hetland cited in this chapter are based on a personal interview and information from his Website at www.globalmissionsawareness.com.

5. Material derived from Eric Pearl's Reconnection Website at www.thereconnection.com and from 2005-2006 conference brochures.

6. Quotes and information about Cal Pierce cited in this chapter are based on a telephone interview and his Website at www.healingrooms.com.

7. Quotes and information about Joe McIntyre cited in this chapter are based on a telephone interview. McIntyre is the author of *E.W. Kenyon and His Message of Faith—The True Story*, which is based on voluminous research of Kenyon's unpublished materials. For more information see www.ifm7.org.

8. Bill Johnson, *When Heaven Invades Earth*. (Shippensburg, PA: Destiny Image Publishers, Inc., 2003), 110. Johnson's books shatter conventional beliefs and build faith. For more information see www.ibethel.org.

* The Vineyard Christian Fellowship movement is an offshoot of the Calvary Chapel movement that originated during the 1960s Jesus People revival in Southern California. John Wimber, former Quaker pastor and Fuller Seminary adjunct professor of Church Growth, assumed leadership of the movement that currently boasts hundreds of churches around the world. For more information about the Vineyard, see their Website, www.vineyardusa.com.

* This information was derived from Sylvia Brown's book, *Prophecy: What the Future Holds For You* (Dutton, Penguin Group, 375 Hudson St., New York, NY July 2004).

* According to the Reiki official Website, http://www.reiki.org/FAQ/WhatIsReiki.html, "Reiki is a Japanese technique for stress reduction and relaxation that also promotes healing. It is administered by 'laying on hands'. The word Reiki is made of two Japanese words—*Rei* which means "God's Wisdom or the Higher Power" and *Ki* which is "life force energy." So Reiki is actually "spiritually guided life force energy."

* According to the Johrei official website,http://www.johrei.com/Spiritual_healing.html, "Johrei is a manifestation of divine energy that can be transmitted through one individual to another for spiritual healing. As the spiritual body is cleansed, the mind and body are also uplifted, healed and attuned to spiritual truth. Johrei has its roots in Japan, and is gaining recognition in the West as a non-invasive energy healing practice. It is a universal vibration that is available to all."

* Wikipedia, the online encyclopedia http://en.wikipedia.org/, wiki/Qigong, defines Qigong as, "an increasingly popular aspect of Chinese medicine involving the coordination of different breathing patterns with various physical postures and motions of the body. Qigong is mostly taught for health maintenance purposes, but there are also some who teach it as a therapeutic intervention."

* Information about John G. Lake is derived from the ministry Website, http://www.johnglake.com.

* Information about E. W. Kenyon is derived from the ministry Website at http://www.kenyons.org For further information about Kenyon, see Joe McIntyre's book, *E.W. Kenyon and His Message of Faith—The True Story*.

PART TWO

CHAPTER 6

Showdown With the Prophets of Baal in the Church

In the days of the prophet Elijah, Israel's kings had slowly succumbed to the influences of the cultures around them, including forming alliances by marrying prominent women of other nations and falling into the worship of their gods. The people of God followed their kings' example. One day they worshiped Yahweh, the Hebrew word for redemptive God. The next day, they would consult the gods of other cultures. As a result of their apostasy, Elijah, under the guiding influence of Yahweh, called forth a drought and a famine ensued. It was a dark time destined to draw the hearts of God's people back to Him.

Ahab and Jezebel ruled over Israel at the time. Ahab considered Elijah a trouble-maker for calling forth the drought and his unwavering devotion to God. Jezebel, a Phoenician, decided to take measures into her own hands and determined that all of Israel should bow down to her Baal—the storm god, the god of rain and sky. Her Baal was sure to release them from the drought. After all, they often called him victorious god; mightiest of heroes; the powerful, excellent one; lord of the fertile land; dispenser of dew, rain and snow; god of the seasons of life; a warrior god. And Asherah, the great goddess,

115

queen of heaven who interceded for Baal, was also a god to be reckoned with. Prophets of both gods could certainly evoke some response if only the people would cooperate, Jezebel reasoned.

She brought 450 prophets of Baal along with 400 prophets of Asherah into the country and placed them on the government payroll. Simultaneously, she slaughtered everyone who was called one of Yahweh's prophets, and persecuted the people of God until they bowed their knees to Baal. Little did she know that Obadiah, their chief of staff, had hidden 100 prophets of God in caves deep within Mt. Carmel. An additional 7,000 people scattered throughout the country had also refused to bow to Baal. A remnant of the people of God was ready to burst onto the scene when it was safe.

For all Elijah knew, he was the only one left who remained loyal to God. His name, in fact, means "my God is the Lord," referring to his loyalty and empowering for his mission—to call the hearts and minds of God's people back to Him. His mission weighed heavily upon him but when the time was right, he gathered his courage and went out to challenge the prophets of Baal to a showdown.

Thousands of people watched as Elijah built an altar and laid a slain bull on top of the wood. He poured water from 12 huge jars onto the sacrifice. No kindling. Wet wood. The challenge to the gods: the god who answers by fire would be the winner, the all powerful one, the victorious god. Only one god could light the match. The first one to do so was the victor.

The prophets of Baal danced their incantations and the prophets of Asherah danced their intercessions. They cut themselves until their blood flowed from their arms and sprayed into the faces of the bystanders as they danced wildly, frantically, invoking their god to act. Elijah taunted them. Perhaps their god was asleep. Or on vacation. Perhaps their god was dead. All the things they had said about Yahweh, Elijah now hurled back in their face.

After awhile, he grew tired of the show, turned toward the people of God and cried out, *How long will you waver between two opinions? If God is God—follow Him!*

116

Then he turned to face the altar and prayed out loud so that the people wouldn't miss the purpose of the showdown. *You are God. I am your servant. Answer me, O God, so these people will know you are turning their hearts back again.*

A bolt of fire from Heaven crackled through the sky, incinerated the bull, the wood, the stones, the soil, and lapped up the water that had run off into a trench. The people stood stunned for a moment, then fell on their faces before the true God—Yahweh. At the command of Elijah, the people seized the prophets of Baal and took them to the valley, to their deaths. (See 1 Kings 18.)

The showdown was over for that day. In the process, Elijah earned respect for the prophetic office and revelatory gifts of God. He stepped into the shifting shadows of loyalty and turned the people's hearts back to the Lord. He symbolically revealed to all of God's people that it isn't enough to hide in a cave or remain quiet about their spiritual beliefs. Total abandonment to the Lord means laying one's life down, on the altar, to be consumed as a living sacrifice. The showdown paved the way for the doors of Heaven to be opened and rain to shower down upon them.

Shifting Shadows of Loyalty Among Christians

The showdown has never ended. Elijah's story depicts the battle for the hearts of God's people that continues today. The Baals of today are not so different—the idols of fertility come packaged in the guise of wealth and materialism; sexual practices that include the use of pornographic images, prostitutes and promotes the sex trade of women and children; and the idols of power come thinly disguised as occult practices that include psychics, mediums, astrology, and divination of various sorts.

By bowing down to the Baals of today, many Christians have become habitations for the enemy and the enemy not only oppresses their thoughts and lives, it permeates the atmosphere in which they worship. This open door to occult influence in the church has resulted in a massive outpouring of confusion, depression, oppression, and anxiety that keeps individuals and churches from reaching their destiny. A case in point follows.

Tom Hauser, pastor of the Vineyard Christian Fellowship in Wilmington, North Carolina, found himself dealing with both Christians and unbelievers who have dabbled in spiritualism and the occult. In the aftermath of their involvement, many could not break free of old thoughts and habits, wrestled with destructive and violent thoughts, and failed to enter into the fullness of salvation. As a result of ministering to them, he developed a training manual and method of bringing freedom to people.

In his manual, *Breaking Free from Darkness: A Practical Guide to Deliverance Ministry*, he writes about Sally's testimony as an example that even Christians dabbling in the shadows of spiritual darkness open themselves to demonic oppression—and that freedom from that bondage doesn't come easily.

A woman I will call "Sally," a church intercessor, came to me asking for prayer. She also informed me that when she tried to pray "in the Spirit" that she would curse violently and expressed that she held great animosity toward her husband. I quickly set an appointment for her to receive ministry.

Sally had been a Christian for nearly 20 years. She was a mother of three, married, and a university professor...she was not only a brilliant individual but she also radiated a sunny personality...By all outward appearances, she seemed perfectly fine.

Sally began by sharing her list of forgiveness items and began her confession process. Soon the Holy Spirit brought forth a revelation through an illustration by my ministry partner and a word-of-knowledge through me. My partner saw a burlap bag full of black seeds of a long-ago time in history; not a modern day image. Simultaneously I heard in my spirit, "generational witchcraft." After sharing this knowledge with Sally, she agreed that she was aware of previous ancestral witchcraft. She went on to inform us that her mother had been a medium. She continued to explain that even while she was a Christian, she had consulted psychics with her mother. However, she indicated that it had occurred several years prior and that she had already asked forgiveness for generational witchcraft and her involvement with psychics. I pressed ahead and asked if she would be willing to renounce these things once again. Even though she felt that she had previously confessed those matters and considered them history and irrelevant, she consented to renouncing her family and ancestor's involvement in witchcraft.

As soon as Sally spoke the words, "I renounce genera..." she arose, glared at me, and started to grab me. I was forced to restrain her to protect myself. She began speaking in a deep, male voice, "She is mine, I am high level and you can't have her."

I spoke back with authority, "I know someone higher than you, His name is Jesus and I have authority over you. You can't have her. She has confessed and you are a trespasser!"

The demonic spirit began to whine, "Where will I go?"

I commanded, "Go to the dry places created by Jesus for you."

The spirit then said, "Ok," and left her.

Finally, Sally, deeply embarrassed, looked at me and began to apologize profusely for what had just taken place...Today she no longer suffers torment.[1]

If the people of God are going to receive the fullness of their spiritual inheritance and experience a greater measure of the presence and power of the Holy Spirit, those who profess to be Christians must choose whom they will serve—God or Baal (the occult spirits and sexual spirits let loose in our world). Elijah's showdown illustrates that there is no room to waver between two choices—God's power is infinitely greater, His ability to guide and comfort and encourage is full of peace and assurance, and His heart is for abundant life. The enemy holds the opposite ability and heart. He maintains his grip on a person's spiritual life, restraining people in shadows and crippling them from entering into the healing light of God's loving presence. Once believers renounce their involvement with the occult, deliverance is assured and they are ready to receive a greater measure of God's presence and power.

In order for the people of God to take their stand in His plan for these last years and generations heralding the second coming of Christ, they must irrevocably renounce any involvement with the occult, be filled with the power of the Holy Spirit, and follow Him. Once the shadows of loyalty no longer darken their understanding, the light of His presence and power will shine more brilliantly through them to the world.

Shifting Shadows of Respect for Prophetic Ministry and Revelatory Gifts

Elijah's prophetic act not only shifted the shadows of loyalty away from the prophets of Baal, it created a newfound respect for the true prophets of God. Elijah was a true prophet endued with the power that comes from true intimacy with the Lord, a bond so close that Elijah received God's authority to single-handedly demolish the power of evil that gripped his people in that place and time. The others who had hidden in caves, perhaps, were only prophets in-training. Yet they no doubt enjoyed a newfound respect when they finally stepped into the light of day.

Standing on a ministry platform is a humbling and often crumbling experience and certainly nothing to be jealous about or to covet. As the prophetic move of God continues to sweep across nations and around the world, many ministers reveal considerable accuracy in prophecy and revelation. Increasingly expressed are the marks of power that come from God with great love, humility, joy, and working in harmony and mutual submission with others for the glory of God. The true prophets are standing the considerable pressures of ministry through the character and grace of God working in them. True prophets take years to develop.

Yet there are those who try to take the fast track to glory and draw attention to the "gifts" they wield. They are often unhealed and unaffirmed people who leave the residue of their state of mind and heart on the lives of their listeners while they attempt to draw glory unto themselves. They are not necessarily false prophets but ones who receive revelation primarily from the source of their own imagination, mind, and soul, and secondarily from the Holy Spirit. Many of them are on their way to becoming true prophets.

Unfortunately, people are not given to respect that process of maturity and revelatory development in young prophets and so they rush to judgment. Frustrated by their lack of recognition or wounded by the judgments leveled against them, many of these young prophets have retreated to caves of spiritual darkness of various sorts—either quitting the ministry, succumbing to depression and emotional breakdowns, or retreating to intellectual rationalizations of why they should no longer pursue the Lord.

Even darker still are those who passed through the shadows blurring the line between authentic revelation from the Holy Spirit and revelation gained through spirits of divination. They either were or have become false prophets who seek revelation from the father of lies for both their own glory and ultimately, satan's.

How do the people of God regain a respect for prophets when many seem so foolish and false compared to ones like Elijah? Elijah's showdown reveals a new level of revelation and power that God wants to unleash upon His people so we may all become revelatory people—enamored with Christ. But first, the people of God need to recognize the differences between true and false prophets in the Church today who call themselves Christian prophets. After all, everyone recognized Elijah as a true prophet. But what about the others—the ones hiding or the ones who had been killed? And where are we in the spectrum of our development as God's revelatory people, completely healed and fully surrendered to the presence and purposes of God?

Regaining a respect for others' ministries entails gaining a true perspective of yourself, the limitations of your spiritual giftedness, and the awareness of how much you depend on God's grace and mercy every day of your life. We all have the same Holy Spirit residing within. And we all have the same obligation to hear from the Lord for ourselves and to act upon what we hear. The marks of power that come from God are based upon the fruit of the Spirit rather than on the judgment of others. The ones who judge the most tend to operate in the least power. Regaining a respect for the prophetic also involves increasing in discernment.

True and False Prophets in the Church

Over the years, powerful ministers have risen in popularity and discovered national and international platforms routinely offered to them. Many in the Church and in the world were captivated with the accurate prophetic insights they shared, their expressions of power to heal and deliver, and their charisma. Along the way, the overwhelming pressures of ministry—personal and spiritual—revealed the fragmentation in some of their hearts and they fell in sexual immorality, drug and alcohol abuse, and spouse abuse. They continued to minister until God and man removed them from public ministry. Because God's gifts are given without repentance, they were able to express the gifts of the Holy Spirit without any of the evidences of God's character or the marks of power that come from God in their lives. Were they false prophets and power brokers or merely foolish ones? How can we discern the difference?

We all come to Christ as broken, immature believers in need of a Savior. Once we meet Him and taste His love, we desire to serve Him. Unfortunately, there are those who taste His love then run with His power before they have time to develop a deep relationship with God and understanding of His ways. Infatuated more with the gifts of God than God Himself, they do not take time to heal from the wounds that brought them to Christ in the first place. It is those wounds and unhealed issues in their lives that undermine their ministry. They become foolish, darkened in their understanding, and many have no one to turn to for help. They started out as authentic believers and prophets interested in using the gifts for the glory of God and the building of His kingdom. However, they ended up as fools.

Rick Joyner, prolific author and prophet, defines the difference between a false prophet and a true one in his book, *The Prophetic Ministry*.

> "There is a simple factor that distinguishes false prophets from the genuine ones. False prophets use their gifts and use other people for their own ends, in order to build up their own influence or ministry. True prophets use their gifts in a self-sacrificing way, for the love of Christ and the sake of His people. Self-seeking, self-promotion, and

self-preservation are the most destructive forces in ministry. Like King Saul, even if we have been anointed by God, we nevertheless can fall into witchcraft if these forces gain control over us."[2]

False prophets who have launched their ministries outside the blessing of God from the very beginning are easiest to spot. Their focus is not on glorifying God or building His Kingdom. They are only interested in themselves.

To obtain spiritual power for the glorification of self is to align with the demonic. Self-glorification is usually evidenced by an over-emphasis on money, seduction, and self-importance. Apparently, foolish prophets may descend in rank to become a false prophet if they fail to heed the warnings of others and continue ministering out of their own unhealed, soulish motivations. Those who operate primarily from a soulish source of revelation are often prone to immorality and using the gift of the Holy Spirit to seduce others. As time goes by, they will opt out of working collaboratively with others. Nor can they work in accountability to others, defer to another's gifts and counsel, and be genuinely glad when another increases in popularity while taking a back seat.

False prophets (and false pastors for that matter) are usually narcissists. For the narcissist doomed to gaze lovingly on his own face, there is no other face than his. No one will be allowed to shine as brightly as he so long as he is in the position of authority. He can only give glory to Jesus when it serves his purposes—paying lip service to the words but displaying little evidence of humility. False prophets or pastors will reach out for any power they can to help them achieve their quest for glory or fulfill their own desires. And spirits of divination are all too willing to respond. Once given over to one demonic power source, other spirits are sure to follow.

True prophets can become false as their brokenness leads them to glorify self, promoting or preserving their ministries beyond the scope of God's intent. They end up using God's power to further their own agendas.

According to Paul Keith Davis, only one question is needed to determine the genuine from counterfeit—"Whose kingdom are they building? Theirs or God's? It's not as hard to distinguish as you think. Just listen to them for a few minutes. It's pretty easy to pick up. If the Lord is really our friend we lay down our life, agenda, ministry, all of our aspirations. Paul was a bondservant."

During an interview, the late Dr. John White, prolific author, New Tribes missionary, and psychiatrist, called this abuse of power a form of apostasy, citing John Owen's exposition of Hebrews 6:4-6.

"Owen maintains that one may operate in all the power of the Holy Spirit, without any of the inward graces of God's character, that is, without being 'saved' at all. You do not have to be a Christian to display spiritual gifts. Non-Christians can display them also, since the Spirit falls on whom He will.

What John Owen says is that you can have the Holy Spirit and still apostatize and you do that because you opt for power rather than for the brightness of the glory of Christ himself. In other words you are not pursuing Christ, you are pursuing power. So it means that on both sides of the Charismatic and Evangelical curtain, there are wheat and tares.

When I first began to understand this I thought, well, what about me? My fear about this personally was countered when Jesus said to me, *He who comes to me I will never reject.* And that filled me with great relief."[3]

Foolish Prophets and Soulish Revelation

What are the marks of revelation that arise from the state of a prophet's soul?

Soulish power—that which originates from a person's state of mind and heart—expresses itself with a variety of mixed markers. Unhealed, unaffirmed people tend to exercise their soulish power to manipulate people and events to compensate for an overwhelming sense of their own powerlessness. Because they have no strong sense of identity or core self rooted in a relationship with Jesus Christ, they are attempting to acquire an external derivation of significance. As a result, when they express the spiritual gifts, the recipients may feel tainted by the residue of soulish imprints. They may be reading your fears and desires, offering pat prophecies common to your demographics, and reflect them back to you as if they are "reading your mail." However, their words will rarely convey the testimony of Jesus to you—who Jesus wants to be for you in this hour, a revelation of His heart toward you, His wisdom, strength, and His counsel.

As Cooke wrote in the Foreword, true prophets live in the light: "When we live in the radiance of God our hearts are captivated by His brilliance. Our focus is sharp, our perceptions in high definition. We are captured by the immensity of the Father."

As for those who are not dwelling in the light, Ezekiel 13:3-6 is careful not to call them false prophets. Instead, he calls them foolish for they prophesy out of their own imaginations or own vanity. *"Woe to the foolish prophets who follow their own spirit and have seen nothing!... Their visions are false and their divinations a lie. They say, 'The Lord declares,' when the Lord has not sent them; yet they expect their words to be fulfilled."* In other words, foolish prophets are not necessarily false prophets. One receiving a prophetic word originating in another's soul power may feel more like the word is mere manipulation or flattery, a put down or a power trip.

As the prophetic movement continues encouraging all believers to become a revelatory people—hearing from God for themselves, many people are moving beyond the foolish stage of spiritual development and into great accuracy.

Discernment, rather than judgment, also needs to increase as we grow into our spiritual inheritance. Many factions in the Charismatic church encourage seeking revelation in your "sanctified imagination" and entering into "throne room experiences" at will. This has become a source of irritation for many who can't seem to access the imaginary realm and confusion for others who just don't know what to make of this teaching.

Much revelation is to be gained through the imagination. Your imagination, based on Scriptural word pictures, can intuit what is really there in the throne room and other rooms and realms of Heaven. Then again, many report actual visions of Heaven's throne room and there are those who have been caught up into Heaven in bodily form. There is a distinct difference. Much of what arises in your imagination is for self-revelation—for healing, encouragement, and creating vision. God is not speaking falsely—just personally. He is drawing out of you what needs to be blessed and affirmed or healed and transformed. If "prophecies" that arise from your imagination are shared as public prophecies, rather than personal insight, they will usually come across as childish attempts to draw attention to self.

The problem with power that originates in the soul—tainted with undealt-with emotions, memories, and traumas—is that it gets in the way of hearing the true voice of the Lord. John Sandford speaks about this jamming of our wavelengths in the *Elijah Task*: "God will never speak falsely but because of who we are we will hear wrongly...both flesh and satan attack one who draws near to God. Few of us enjoy the honeymoon of God's love long before the flesh and the enemy begin to jam our wavelengths."[4]

Sandford knows from personal experience that no one will graduate from the Lord's school of listening with his pride intact. Most budding prophets and revelatory people will end up looking like a fool but it does not make them a false prophet. The pressures on Sandford as a young pastor at the beginning of his prophetic ministry, coupled with exhaustion, resulted in a strong spiritual delusion. During a progressive series of visions he became completely convinced that God had revealed the exact time of the rapture. It was to occur the afternoon of the day he was preaching at a ministry school involving Agnes Sandford. Agnes, a true mother in the prophetic, promptly urged him to stop talking and sent him to bed. He woke the next day feeling more refreshed and more than a little bit embarrassed. He explained what happened:

> "I became caught up in over-serious mysticism, confusing that with true faith...I became overburdened, overtired, carried away with visions and insights, and finally deluded. Satan's delight is to come to someone who is enjoying a true spiritual experience and then help him go too far.

> "I needed that strong spiritual delusion because my confidence had been in my ability to hear God, not in God's ability to overcome my sinful heart to speak to me.

"And as I saw my idolatry more clearly, I had to die to all such seeing, and be careful not to cherish insight more than the Lord."[5]

The psychological health of the prophet determines the impact of his or
her state of mind or soul about the gift. A true prophet will bear the marks of
the power of God, the nature of God, and the fruit of the Spirit over time.
They will work collaboratively and in accountability to others, learning from
their mistakes and growing in humility. Unhealed prophets will bear the
marks of their own brokenness. If the Church fails to reach out to them, leaving them to smolder in despair, unrepentant sin, and brokenness, they may
succumb to the influence of occult power.

The Spirit of Divination

Many Christians dismiss prophet ministers stating that they are all operating in prophetic gifts that are empowered by a spirit of divination. Prophets
generally agree that the spirit of divination can impact both those who are not
Christians and those who are. Prophets, having a heightened sensitivity to the
spiritual realm and all that resides within it, are not immune to receiving revelation from spirits of divination. Once recognizing their error, true prophets
will back away, listen to the Lord and continue to glorify Jesus in a spirit of
humility. False prophets, continuing to operate by demonic revelation, will
eventually become undone. God will mercifully expose the motives of their
hearts in hopes that they will take advantage of opportunities to heal and mature in their gifting. If they persist, having opened themselves to the influence
of the demonic, they will become undone by the one whose mission is to rob,
kill, and destroy…to deceive even the elect.

The spirit of divination referred to in Acts 16:16-18, is derived from the
Greek word "Puthon." In Greek mythology, Puthon refers to the Pythian
serpent, or dragon, that was said to have guarded the oracle at Delphi. The
Greeks used this term to describe soothsayers and diviners. This *python*
spirit, or spirit of divination, inhabits a young slave girl. Under the influence
of this spirit, she was a walking psychic hotline and brought her masters
much profit. This spirit of divination impacts not only today's psychics and
mediums, but slithers its way into the minds of many Christians, tempting

them to peer into where God has not invited and staunchly defend their revelations as oracles of God irregardless of source and accuracy.

According to Mahesh Chavda, a pastor with an international reputation as a miracle worker who has ministered extensively in third world countries: People with a spirit of divination may say some things that are true and demonstrate knowledge they could not otherwise know. The Holy Spirit will give us discernment regarding whether such a spirit is present. One way to tell the difference is that genuine prophecy, because it comes from the Holy Spirit, will always glorify Jesus; a spirit of divination will not.[6]

Kris Vallotton believes that once a spirit of divination is discerned and cast out, the individual will no longer be able to prophesy. After preaching one evening, a woman asked to see him. She was dressed in a three-piece business suit—quite unusual for rural Redding, California. During their conversation she claimed to be a psychic who worked with executives of corporations to help guide them in their decision making processes. A friend referred her to the church in hopes that she could find relief from her sleep disorder. For the past year, the woman could not sleep, feeling spiritually tormented through-out the night. Apparently, her friend had come to the church and received healing for the same condition.

Not one to waste time, Kris said, "That spirit guide that speaks to you is a demon. In fact you have two spirit guides. Your gift is from them but they also want to kill you. In order to help your torment I have to ask the demons to leave."

She thought for a moment then replied, "If you make the spirit guides leave will I be able to foretell the future?"

"No," Kris said.

"So, if you make my spirit guides leave I won't be able to guide those corporations. Then I won't have a business."

"It's really simple," Kris replied. "You can be rich and tormented, or peaceful and broke."

She closed her eyes and thought about it for several minutes, then said, "I'd rather be broke and peaceful."

"Here is the deal. I'll ask the spirit guides to leave but you'll have to ask Jesus to come into your life in order for them to leave." To Kris' surprise, she agreed and invited Jesus into her life, renounced a few things, asked forgiveness for obtaining guidance from wrong spirits. Then, she fell under the power of God and lay on the floor for at least a half hour. Before she left, she told Kris that she had never felt so much peace in her life.[7]

Discerning the spirit of divination operating in a non-Christian's life seems to be fairly easy. Discerning the same spirit operating in a true prophet's life is a bit more difficult.

During the prophetic movement of the late 1980s, many prophets were accused of ministering from occult sources of divination. Their prophetic words about people's pasts, their current situations and future destinies drew people hungry for affirmation and direction. In a sense, the needs of the people caused many ministers to react like psychics.

According to John Sandford,

"Prophets were in demand and people came in rudely jostling each other for seats hoping to get a word. I don't know if the prophets were as aware as they should have been but importunity can defile your receptors. Importunity turned the prophets into diviners. People were pushing them that way.

"God may decide to reveal to a prophet what will happen in the future or what has happened in the past. That is God's revelation, but satan copies all things and it's a short distance from listening to the Lord receptively and out of intimacy with him to striving to hear. When we strive to hear we can give out what isn't from God. Divination is to peer where God has not invited.

"I don't think they are aware when they are doing it but afterward if their conscience bothered them, they became aware as the Holy Spirit convicted them."[8]

The prophetic movement continues to mature. Most prophets take care when addressing public prophecy to the corporate church. They also guard their hearts a little better and don't allow others' needs to push them into attempts to gain revelation through either soulish readings and intuitions of individuals or from a spirit of divination. As Sandford revealed, just because someone with authentic revelatory gifts crosses the line into divination, it does not necessarily mean they stay there and become false prophets.

As the prophetic movement grows, there seems to be less emphasis on promoting solo practitioners who only see and hear in part, and more upon corporate hearing and accountability structures. Those accountability structures include C. Peter Wagner's Apostolic Council of Prophetic Elders; regional and national prophetic roundtables; and other efforts to increase collaboration, mutual deference to one another's giftings, and discernment in local churches.

For pastors worldwide called to shepherd all the budding revelatory people in their midst, discernment and wisdom will be increasingly necessary in the days to come. They will need to recognize that a suspected false prophet may be merely a fool who can be redeemed. A foolish prophet may yet become a great prophet. And the truly false prophets and those operating from occult power sources need to be dealt with before they cause confusion or division and harm the Church.

Shifting Shadows of Greed in the Church

When Elijah's showdown put an end to the prophets of Baal and Asthoreth, the people of God were forced to take a look at how those false gods had infiltrated not only their hearts, but their culture as well. In fact, Elijah was so concerned about it that the Lord had to speak to him specifically, telling him that 7,000 people remained loyal and refused to kiss Baal. (See 1 Kings 19:18.) Although this can be interpreted in many ways, the confusing kiss of worship, laced with betrayal, was revealed through one key character in Jesus' day. Fertility gods promised increasing harvest, wealth, and prestige. Their shadows linger in the communities of today's Christians in the form of the Judas kiss.

According to Paul Keith Davis, during this season heralding the close of this age, greed in the form of the Judas kiss will be confronted as more Christians allow light to penetrate the shadows that have crept into the Church.

"In Isaiah 14:14, the great "I will" of satan—I will make myself like the most high—is the most dangerous spirit of all. This spirit will manifest itself in people almost like the genuine thing, but the heart of it is darkness. A type of that is Judas. He was one of the 12 apostles, casting out demons and healing the sick, but not one person discerned who he was until the very end.

Judas was the son of perdition—a type of the most dangerous spirit of all—darkness at his source.

Judas always had the money bag, always slipped his hand into the money bag, and would sell out his friends for more money. I'm not against the Church having prosperity, but the ones who have money as their motivation for ministry are not going to be advancing God's Kingdom.

Jesus said satan would deceive the very elect if possible. Satan currently functions in the Church and many people don't recognize it. Psychics don't even pretend to give God the glory or acknowledge the Holy Spirit. But Christians should. Judas was among the believers, gifted and anointed alongside them up to the point of being filled with the Holy Spirit. But he couldn't be filled with the Holy Spirit. Many people among us cannot be filled with the Holy Spirit because they are filled with the spirit of antichrist. The Lord says, *The spirit of antichrist has crept in among you—clouds without rain—but there is no rain* (Jude 1:12).

The appearance of those given over to this spirit is so close to that of real spirit-filled believers, that it will take true spiritual discernment to separate the two. I don't know yet that there are enough people functioning in prophetic maturity to discern and confront those spirits.[9]

How many ministries have flourished by twisting Scriptures into prosperity *get rich by sending me your money* messages? How many prophets have prophesied for money? Elijah remained in the desert during the famine, eating the same meal over and over, utterly dependant on the God of miracles and the grace extended by a lowly widow…just one widow…not hundreds.

In the process, he demonstrated a level of faith and purity that is also demonstrated by true prophets and ministers who live in famine-ravished lands. It is a level of dependency on the Lord that may also be required of those who live in more prosperous countries in the days to come. We may all be called to step into the firestorm of total surrender and dependency.

Embracing the Firestorm of Total Surrender

Everyone watching Elijah knew the significance of his altar. They knew that the fire from Heaven consumed not only a bull, but themselves; not only the wood, but everything they had built their lives upon and all their carnal reasoning. Not only stones, but every corporate, tribal, and church affiliation supporting their identity; not only soil, but all the withered seed of weeds, doubt, and unbelief, hidden in the ground that might spring to life in the coming rains. Even the water of past moves of the Holy Spirit was being consumed; every lingering drop evaporated in the fire. It was a firestorm resulting in the complete annihilation of who they thought themselves to be. It burned so hot that there were no ashes. The only thing left to see was the stunning glory of God shining in all His brilliance, driving back the shadows from the land.

The meaning of the sacrifice, simply put, was all about the purification of His beloved people. Fire not only purifies but transforms individuals into anointed people of God, faces reflect His light, hearts focus solely on Him, destinies are fulfilled in His power. The God who answers by fire—He is God...we are not.

Elijah's invitation to embrace the firestorm of total surrender confronts us today. The showdown between the influences of Baal in our lives and the influences of the Holy Spirit are coming to a point when we must irrevocably cease wavering between two opinions that create shifting shadows of loyalty within us. If God is God, we must follow Him. In the words of apostle Paul:

Therefore I urge you, brothers, in view of God's mercy, to offer your bodies as living sacrifices, holy and pleasing to God—this is your spiritual act of worship. Do not conform any longer to the pattern of this world, but be transformed by the renewing of your mind. Then you will be able to test and approve what God's will is—His good, pleasing and perfect will (Romans 12:1-2).

Paul urges us to become like the one you behold—Jesus—in whom there is no shadow of turning from intimacy with the Father and fulfillment of His purpose. We cannot separate the shadows of society until we have separated them within ourselves. We cannot release the fullness of the light of the world until that light shines more purely within us. We must all renounce past occult involvement, operating from soulish sources of revelation, and bowing down to kiss the Baals of this age. We are being called to die as a beloved child of God on the altar of total surrender.

As we offer ourselves upon the altar receive healing and step into our inheritance as the beloved of God, a firestorm is sure to be loosed in the days to come. Many prophets believe that the past moves of the Holy Spirit will pale in comparison to the sense of His presence and power that God is preparing to reveal. Indeed, we are already seeing signs of that increase all over the world, small tokens of what is to come. During this time we find a hint in Elijah's story that *those who cling to worthless idols forfeit the grace that could be theirs.* [10] Those who submit to the purifying power of His outrageous love now—will leap into this coming move with joy.

ENDNOTES

1. Tom Hauser, *Breaking Free from Darkness—A Practical Guide to Deliverance.* (Wilmington, NC: Vineyard Community Church), 5-6.

2. Joyner, *Prophetic Ministry,* 98.

3. Quotes derived from a personal interview with the late Dr. John White, prolific author, psychiatrist, and missionary, a few years prior to his death. Previously published in the article, "Supernatural ministry," by Julia Loren, *Renewal Journal* #10 (97:2): *Evangelism,* at www.renewaljournal.com.

4. Sandford, *Elijah Task,* 155-56.

5. Ibid., 202.

6. Chavda, *Power of the Blood*, 146.

7. Quotes and information about Kris Vallotton cited in this chapter are derived from a telephone interview.

8. Quotes and information about John Sandford cited in this chapter are derived from a personal interview. More of this interview was published in *Charisma* magazine, September 2005.

9. Based on a telephone interview with Paul Keith Davis.

10. Jonah 2:8.

CHAPTER 7

Showdown With the Prophets of Baal in the World

Elijah's fiery showdown destroyed the prophets of Baal in residence but it did not eradicate the worship of Baal or destroy the temple of Baal and idolatry throughout the land. Elijah ascended into Heaven knowing that his burden had passed to another generation. Years later, his prophetic successor Elisha named Jehu king over Israel, a pronouncement that launched Jehu on a little road trip in his chariot. Jehu's first stop confronted Ahab's lineage with the words, "How can there be peace as long as all the idolatry and witchcraft of your mother Jezebel abound?" He then killed the kings of Israel and Judah who had arisen after Ahab died. His second stop pitched Jezebel to her death. Then he finished off Ahab's 70 sons, in a sense, fulfilling all of the prophesies Elijah had spoken against the house of Ahab for their idol worship. Yet Jehu had one more task to fulfill before sitting down to his kingdom-building duties. He created a plan that deceptively invited the prophets of Baal to a great feast, a barbecue, a sacrifice—and they were the ultimate guests of honor. (See 2 Kings 9-10.)

While the prophets of Baal attended to their sacrifices and burnt offerings, Jehu ordered the guards to kill them.

So they cut them down with the sword. The guards and officers threw the bodies out and then entered the inner shrine of the temple of Baal. They brought the sacred stone out of the temple of Baal and burned it. They demolished the sacred stone of Baal and tore down the temple of Baal, and the people have used it as a latrine to this day. So Jehu destroyed Baal worship in Israel (2 Kings 10:25-28).

Fast forward to today and we see another showdown emerging—a showdown against the same principalities, the archetypes of power, that emerged so strongly during the reign of Ahab and Jezebel. God has been raising up many prophetic leaders to train others to participate in the showdown. Jehu's "guards and officers" of today go into the streets armed with the sword of the Spirit, which is the Word of God, and the power of the Spirit to love and redeem the lost prophets of today's Baal worship...those caught up in the occult.

George Otis, author of a comprehensive study of why darkness and evil resides in specific places of the world more than others, has much to say about spiritual power. He believes some people are afraid and unprepared to deal with the mysteries of power and writes, "Having little firsthand experience with the supernatural, they are inclined to shy away from its mysteries."[1] He also encourages Christians to become more aware of what surrounds us and become better prepared to deal with it.

"The modern appetite for spiritual power, whatever its source, is no less ravenous. We have only to look at the unprecedented popularity of paranormal television programming, the proliferation of New Age teaching, and the revitalization of various indigenous religions. People want power, and the enemy is very willing to oblige.

"Since demonic signs and wonders will increase as we edge closer to the Second Coming of Christ, we face some critical questions: Are we prepared? Do we have the necessary battlefield experience to stand up to this expanding competition? For many believers, including some in positions of ministry leadership, the answer is a resounding, 'No.'"[2]

Last Days' Showdown Between the Powers

Many prophets agree that we are nearing the close of this age and that a cataclysmic clash of power is on the horizon. Indeed, we are already seeing signs of it. No one speaks to this coming battle as eloquently as Dr. Bill Hamon, founder of Christian International Ministries Network based in Florida and contemporary prophet:

> It is God's pleasure and purpose to demonstrate His power and glory in these last days. The Church is entering its time to demonstrate God's Kingdom on Earth. It is time for the Church to start praying and fulfilling Jesus' directive prayer for His Will to be done on earth as it is in Heaven.

> The conflicts of the ages are upon us now. The battle between the Body of Christ and the antichrist is being engaged to the extent that it will be demonstrated on international television and the Internet.

> We are entering the days of Moses and Elijah. Just as Moses demonstrated God's power against Pharaoh and all of his false gods, even so today God wants to demonstrate His power again. In Romans 9:17 and Exodus 9:16 God declares of Pharaoh, *"For this very purpose I have raised you up that I may show My power in you, and that My name may be declared in ALL THE EARTH."* (NKJV) In Exodus 10:12 God said He wanted to show His signs and demonstrate His power against Pharaoh so that all Israel and their descendants would know that Jehovah is the One and only true and Almighty God.

> Elijah confronted the prophets of Baal on Mt. Carmel. He demonstrated that Jehovah was the only true God with power that no man or demon power could match. The magicians of Pharaoh could duplicate Moses' rod turning into a snake, water into blood, and brought frogs up. However they could not make dust into lice or match any of the remaining demonstrations of God's power. When Elijah, the true prophet of God, challenged the false prophets of Baal they could do no great signs and wonders.

Demonic power demonstrations are reduced to almost nothing when facing a true and powerful prophet of God.

My daughter had a dream a few years ago. She saw some true prophets of God on a television show challenging some occultist representative. There will be demonstrations and contests between God's true prophets and the false occultic and antichrist prophets. One of my pastors, who is a prophet, set up a booth at a New Age/psychic fair. Everyone else was charging a fee for psychic readings but he put up a sign the read "free spiritual readings." He and his team gave accurate prophecies with specific words of knowledge. Several witch doctors, satanists, and psychic leaders got saved and filled with the Holy Spirit. They experienced the superiority of God's power and insight over their own powers.

It is time for the Church, especially the prophets and apostles, to demonstrate that Jesus Christ is the only true and loving God. [3]

Prophet Jim Goll, founder of Encounters Network, also believes that an army of prophets of God are being called and trained to stand up to the demonic spirits driving our modern day Baal worshipers and bring the presence and power of God into the battle for their souls. According to Goll:

"There is coming upon the scene of time a great conflict of paramount proportions. It is the Battle of the Prophets—those who are true soldiers of the cross of Jesus Christ and those who flaunt the boastful pride of man mixed with New Age false Spiritism and who wag big egos.

"The end result is clear to those who truly know the Word of God and the God of the Word. Humble yet bold prophets of the One True God shall prevail in the Last Days by their testimony of the power of the blood of Him who saves even against atheist, secular, and demonic humanism in the last days." [4]

As this showdown occurs the shifting shadows of confusion will give way to increasing darkness. Light always pierces the darkness and chases away the shadows. According to Mahesh Chavda, "The dark will get darker but glory will get thicker. If we will look to Jesus, He is going to anoint his Church as never before. And we will arise and shine."[5]

John Sandford also believes a greater revelation of God's light and power are going to be seen in the coming days. "I believe a revelation of God is coming that is beyond our realities, not His reality, our reality outside the bounds of what we think. It will call for flexibility, willingness to die to ourselves, and at the same time it, will call for stability. The Church will not look like what we've seen in past years. It is going to change rapidly."[6]

Part of that changing face of the Church includes an increased understanding of a revelation of God's love and power that we have never seen before. Rather than just knowing the healing and prophetic power and feeling glimpses of the tangible presence of God, the Church may discover who God really is—a reality outside the bounds of our limited imagination and understanding of Scripture. Once captivated by that intimate revelation of the face of God, we will all be transformed. Then, we will all be called to embrace the supernatural more fully—the revelation of Heaven and earthly matters that comes through increasing spiritual experiences and signs and wonders breaking through the heavens that defies all scientific rationalizations and explanations.

Rick Joyner speaks to both the coming increase in supernatural power and the coming responsibility to definitively answer the question that Elijah presented to the people of His day: *How long will you waver between two opinions?*

As we proceed toward the conclusion of this age, the conflict between light and darkness will become increasingly supernatural. The day when it was possible to take a neutral stance toward the supernatural is over. If we do not know the true power of God's Spirit, we will become increasingly subject to the power of the evil one. Those whose fears or doctrines have led them to avoid even the Lord's supernatural power will soon find themselves and their children easy prey for evil supernatural powers.[7]

Following the Leaders

Patricia King and Stacey Campbell of Kelowna, British Columbia, Canada, are among the prophets who take the prophetic power and love of God to the streets—confronting the effects of the occult influences in North American cultures. They call it Extreme Prophetic. They also take teams of ordinary Christians-turned-prophets—students, housewives, and businessmen—into the streets of major cities, where the light of Christ invades the darkness around them. Some of their work is documented on King's Extreme Prophetic television show.

In one episode, the camera reveals the eyes of a man hardened by anger, vestiges of prison life still marking his face, as he listens to Extreme Prophetic team members on the streets of Las Vegas. The man in this segment had walked out of prison just hours before team members stopped him on the sidewalk outside a casino and told him that God loved him and had a plan for his life. Tears ran down the man's face when pastor and prophetic minister Stacey Campbell, co-founder with her husband Wesley Campbell of Revival Now ministry and Be a Hero ministry, shared prophetic insights about child-hood events that had filled the man with anger—events she could not have known about. He accepted Christ there on the street, virtually unconscious of the cameras that would spread his testimony around the world.

King, the woman behind Extreme Prophetic, is a hip and extroverted 50-something grandmother who lives with her husband in Kelowna, about a three-hour drive from Vancouver. Saved in the 1970s after practicing the oc-cult, then serving as a missionary with Youth With A Mission, King has be-come known as a Bible teacher who emphasizes prayer, evangelism, and the gifts of the Holy Spirit.

She credits a 1994 visit to the Toronto Blessing renewal with spawning both a storm of questions and some "amazing" spiritual experiences that mo-tivated her to dig deeper in prayer and Bible study. The result was a teaching series about biblical encounters with a supernatural God. She later founded a "glory school" and wrote a few books including, *Third Heaven, Angels and Other Stuff*.

King believes supernatural encounters should be taken to the streets. "[People] are not hungry for institutionalized religion; they are hungry for true encounters with God," King said. "The whole idea behind the Extreme Prophetic School is to take God's prophetic gift with extreme love into extreme places—anywhere and everywhere the unsaved congregate."[8]

While Patricia King naturally gravitated toward ministry to those in the occult, Stacey Campbell, a pastor's wife, had to push past her own judgments of those who had been involved in the occult before she moved outside the walls of the church to venture into the streets. A brief conversation with a man in Brisbane, Australia, challenged her thinking and set her on a new course of ministry. The man told Campbell that he had become a Christian at a psychic fair, a fair he attended because he knew he was looking for God.

According to Campbell, "I never thought people were looking for God at psychic fairs. The general opinion of the church is that these people are demonized so we create an unknown judgment about them with our beliefs. They are hungry for spirituality and they want the real thing. So I asked this man to tell me about what happened at the fair."[9]

The pastor of the Australian church had heard about a psychic fair coming to town and the church thought they would be proactive in outreach rather than judgment. Eight months prior to the scheduled fair, they sent intercessors to the site and prayed. In the meanwhile, the pastors trained people in the art of listening to God and releasing prophecy and they rented a booth so they could have a presence onsite. During the psychic fair, intercessors surrounded the area and their booth and prayed. As a result, they noticed the line at psychics' booths got shorter and shorter. The line at prophet's booth grew longer. Participants at the fair, both curious and already given over to the dark lord's counterfeit powers, gravitated toward the light, love, and purity of power emanating form the church's prophetic booth. This new Christian was one of those who stood in line at the booth and received not only a word of love and destiny, he received Christ as his Savior, renouncing his infatuation with the idols of power in his culture.

As Stacey listened, the Lord opened her heart to minister beyond the confines of the church sanctuary. "Suddenly the Lord said, 'I want you to do that.' Now, I'm a pastor's wife—I've never been outside the church. The more I tried to argue against stepping out to prophesy to people involved with the occult and on the streets, the worst it sounded. Finally, I read in First Corinthians that prophecy is for the unbeliever—not necessarily for the believer."

She talked to her friend Patricia King about launching a prophet's booth of some sort in their community of Kelowna. She suggested a "Spiritual Readings" booth and the two women led several Extreme Prophetic students to the local Booster Juice where they hung a sign outside the door stating "FREE spiritual readings." According to Campbell, the experience changed her mind about how pervasive the draw of the occult is in North America and the need for Christians to meet people on the streets and interrupt that draw toward the dark powers that roam about freely looking for ones to devour.

> "I had two fears about this Booster Juice set up: that no one would show up, and that someone would show up and we would have to prophesy. I discovered that it was the most effective form of evangelism I have ever done in my life. I've been through a variety of techniques including Campus Crusade, door-to-door, survey evangelism, and preaching on the streets. Setting up the draw toward Spiritual Readings was so much more effective because the hungry and the lost come searching for you.

> "The lost lined up at the door from the very first day. Within the first half hour of opening, people stood in line for about 30 minutes until they could sit down with one of the teams of two—one who would sit quietly and intercede while the other one prophesied. We would start by explaining that we were Christians and we believed God would speak to them.

> "As we began to prophesy in their life and address the wounds in their life, many were visibly moved. Several were saved and several later came to church."

Despite the spiritual openness, Campbell also sees opposition to their work on the streets coming from both secular and from churched individuals.

"Wherever the power of God goes it clashes with kingdom of darkness. In cultures where the awareness of the spiritual is heightened there seems to be more of a kingdom clash. Here, we do see various degrees of hostility or harassment against what we are doing. We see that the clash is sometimes more demonstrable and sometimes lighter...meaning there is not a full-on manifestation of a demon in the one harassing us.

"Also, a lot of churches may have a fear-based reaction, not understanding the power of prophetic and healing evangelism. Really the biblical paradigm reveals this form of evangelism as normal Christianity wherever you go. Our current cultural understanding is that most of Christianity takes place in buildings rather than outside. So, many Christians see what we're doing as an occultist practice rather than as normal Christianity. We all actually have a biblical mandate to go out in the power of the Holy Spirit, preaching the word with signs following and bringing light into the darkness.

"From the beginning of time God has been after the whole wide world. It is purposed in God's heart that every gift, whether mercy or hospitality or any other, is not supposed to be used only to the church but also taken out to continue to expand the kingdom. Take every gift, a service gift, to serve the bride and the world. This mercy movement of prophetic evangelism is the natural outcome of the prophetic movement."

Doug Addison, founder of InLight Connection and a prophetic evangelist whose ministry is based in the Los Angeles area of California has regularly taken Christians to New Age events, infiltrated the notorious Burning Man desert gatherings by setting up spiritual readings and dream interpretation booths, and generally showed up where few Christians dare to tread. Burning Man is an annual experiment in temporary community dedicated to radical self-expression and self-reliance, i.e., people wear all manner of costumes or nothing at all, consume drugs or not. Although it is a commercial-free event, a variety of people offer their own spiritual insights and smorgasbord of occultic information to one another. While it started as a private beach party in San

Francisco where a couple of men decided to build a wooden man and burn him on the beach as a form of self-expression, it has grown to include thousands of people who camp in the sweltering heat of Nevada's Black Rock desert over Labor Day weekend. The event culminates in the burning of a giant human effigy. Participants call it an experiment in survival, due to having to camp in such extreme heat, completely dependent on what supplies they bring and share. Between the heat and the burning of the giant wooden man, it seems almost as if the demonic realm taunts participants into unconsciously living out a version of surviving a mild hell—perhaps a trial run for many.

Addison believes, like Campbell and King, that the logical outflow of the contemporary Christian prophetic movement is destined for the streets. And as prophetic believers move out, the Holy Spirit will move in and release even greater measures of accuracy and power encounters. According to Addison:

"I think that one of the next powerful moves of God will occur among those caught up in the New Age. I think it will be on the level of the early Book of Acts where they met everyday and no one dared join them because they were operating in such a high level of power. Someone will stand against us and we will actually be able to do greater things than they are doing. Witches can currently pin people against the wall. I think we will be able to do greater things. When we walk by their booths at New Age shows, they lose their power. We don't pray for them to shut down, we pray that their gifts would be pointed in the right direction and answer the call of God on their life. When we go around blessing people, their power shuts down. One group thought we were psychic vampires because every time we walked by they would lose their power. Another group liked our light and energy and that good things began to happen when we were in the area.

"The pagan burning man groups are more the radical raw end of the New Age [movement]. This year, Burning Man was the best ever. Our spiritual readings and dream interpretation tent resulted in a couple dozen salvations. There was a 30-minute line to get into the dream tent. Lots of people who came in would say they didn't want to be a Christian because they had been so wounded by the church but admitted that they loved Jesus.

"At Burning Man our booth was voted the camp with the best 'Karma.' They actually gave a spirituality award to Christians!

"We don't advertise that we're Christians. We go in and are sensitive to them, telling them more about themselves, giving them prophesies, and releasing deliverance prayers. We actually ask them, 'Would you mind if we ask the Creator to remove anything that might hinder you from reaching your destiny?'

"At Burning Man we also ask the person if he or she would like a spiritual cleansing or dream interpretation. We just gather as a group and the Holy Spirit touches them to the point of tears. Some demons leave. I see power encounters all the time.

"Second Corinthians 4:4 states that the god of this age has blinded the minds of unbelievers. They lack discernment. Our job is to open their eyes to new experiences in God. Acts 26:17-18 reads *I am sending you to them to open their eyes*...that eye-opening experience is required to release many from the demonic through demonstrations of God's love and power."[10]

Addison is quick to reveal that not every encounter is a God encounter—meaning that he doesn't presume to minister to everyone who comes along his path—either at New Age fairs or on the street. As light infiltrates the darkness, the shadows of confusion harass demonized people and propel them toward Addison and others who minister on the street.

"If someone walks up to me on the street and they engage me—they are probably sent by the demonic spirit harassing them. I won't engage on the defense. If I did engage and God hadn't called me to, God would have mercy. But as you mature, you don't presume that you have to unleash God to everyone who walks in front of you; if you do, what happens is backlash, not a good encounter. When I see someone coming I ask the Holy Spirit immediately, 'Is this something you want me to do?'

Dark Lord Defeat Through Agape Revolution

What if God moved sovereignly in the New Age movement, calling individuals to Himself in the way that He did during the Jesus People movement when thousands of hippies in the 1960s and 1970s came to Jesus out of a purple haze of billowing marijuana smoke and drugs, free love, and naked meanderings through rock concerts and forest glens?

What if God released an army of angels to point their swords at the hearts of those who have rejected Jesus as just another teacher, and pierce them with the truth? Would we have eyes to see who Jesus is raising up at this hour in history? Will we accept those who step out of the shadows from the kingdom of darkness into the Kingdom of light? Will we be prepared to answer their questions about the difference between occult power and the power of the blood of Jesus and the Holy Spirit? Or will judge them and encourage them to leave our presence?

And if these individuals step away from occult power, then start expressing the gifts of the spirit with greater power than we have seen in our minds, will we bless them or seek to shut them down? God is releasing the fullness of His Holy Spirit and the Spirit will fall on whomever He wills it. Will we bless their accelerated process of discipleship and keep our hands off their zeal and anointing as the love of God consumes them and sends them out into the world? If we do, the world will gravitate toward the burning man or woman in their midst. If we don't, our religion will kill their zeal and all that will remain is a habitation for the enemy.

Not only did Doug Addison hear the stories of many caught up in the New Age and occult who had been wounded and rejected by the church, he also felt rejected by church members because of his giftedness. Yet he persevered in his spiritual growth and in the process of healing the wounds that drove him toward the occult. Despite the rejection of Christians, he is now one of satan's greatest enemies, and ministers in churches around the nation, training others in the ways of prophetic evangelism.

Some, like a television psychic who attended Addison's church meetings for a year before deciding not to accept Christ because she would lose her television show, are blatantly involved with occult activity. Yet, because of Addison's acceptance of her, this same psychic inadvertently led several people to the Lord when she encouraged them to attend Addison's meetings. Others are more naive about the origins and differences between God's power and psychic power. But one of the most interesting facts about many people caught up in New Age teachings is that those seeking answers from the occult are also drawn to the light of Christ and the power that flows from Spirit-filled believers. Sometimes, it takes patience rather than power encounters to reveal the fullness of God's love.

One of Randy Clark's Global Awakening ministry team members attending a meeting in Brazil met a tall, young woman who appeared more refined than the average Brazilian attending the meetings held in a huge Assembly of God church building in Imperatriz. She was an English teacher who had come to help as an interpreter. At the end of the meeting on the first night the ministry team member sensed that she was not a Christian and asked her what church she attended. "Oh, I am Catholic but I attend other meetings," she replied. "How do you say *spiritualisme*? It is more a philosophy. It is Christian. Do you know the teachings of Allan Kardac, a French philosopher? His teachings are sweeping through Brazil, becoming very popular." [11]

Allan Kardac, a French educator and philosopher, started investigating the paranormal manifestations of spiritualism occurring in America and Europe in 1854. He is to Europe what Blavatsky was to America spiritualism—the first to write down extensive volumes of teachings that serve as the foundation for the New Age movement in Europe and South America. Through extensive interviews with spirits channeled through mediums, Kardac codified spiritualist teaching for all of Europe. His influence is most felt in Brazil today, where the uneducated masses gravitate toward Macumba witchcraft—a combination of Catholicism, African witchcraft, and spiritism—for healing and spirituality, and the more educated masses are shifting away from Catholicism and into Kardac's brand of spiritism.

Kardac's followers believe spiritism is a philosophy that is Christian because it has *the moral transformation of mankind* as its finality. It advocates a return to the teachings of Jesus Christ in our daily lives but denies Jesus' atonement. Instead, successive lives lived out through reincarnation provide our own means of atonement for our sins. It attempts to show Christianity in its "true expression of love and charity" yet it also believes that heaven and hell are absurd concepts and that in channeling spirits we receive a fuller picture of the meaning of life. Kardac's teachings also embrace scientific reasoning—which appeals to many intellectuals—and the laying on of hands for healing. His teachings are no different from many teachings of spiritualists in North America.

The ministry team member encouraged the English teacher to test the spirits next time she attended a spiritualist meeting and talked with her about the difference between Kardac's Christianity and true Christianity. The next night, the ministry team member could tell that she was moved by the willingness of the North American team to pray for the Brazilians, and even more amazed by the power of God lovingly touching and healing many who came forward for prayer. So, at the end of the evening, the team member prayed for her and watched as she too encountered the love and peace she was looking for. By the end of their time together, the team member had written down several Scriptures and gave them to her—knowing that as a true seeker of the truth, the Truth would set her free. She received not only a sense of the true power of God but a sense of the meaning of Agape love. She had been drawn to Clark's Charismatic meetings because her spiritualist meetings could not meet the deep needs in her heart. The next time she attended a spiritualist meeting, she promised that she would test the spirits in accordance with 1 John 4:1-6:

> *Dear friends, do not believe every spirit, but test the spirits to see whether they are from God, because many false prophets have gone out into the world. This is how you can recognize the Spirit of God: every spirit that acknowledges that Jesus Christ has come in the flesh is from God, but every spirit that does not acknowledge Jesus is not from God. This is the spirit of the antichrist, which you have heard is coming and even now is already in the world. You, dear children, are from God and have already overcome them, because the one who is in you is greater than the one who is in the world. They are from the world and*

therefore speak from the viewpoint of the world, and the world listens to them. We are from God, and whoever knows God listens to us; but whoever is not from God does not listen to us. This is how we recognize the Spirit of truth and the spirit of falsehood.

She also agreed that she didn't want to be deceived and would ask if Kardac's teaching includes Jesus as the Christ, our Savior, who made atonement for our sins and is the only way to the Father and Heaven in accordance with 1 John 2:22:

Who is the liar? It is the man who denies that Jesus is the Christ. Such a man is the antichrist—he denies the father and the son.

In her search for authentic spirituality, she knew her heart longed for peace and love more than intellectual reasoning. Before she could surrender to Jesus, she needed an experience of His love and peace as well as insight into what the Bible really teaches about the person of Jesus Christ, rather than the philosophy behind Jesus' teachings. She wasn't ready to receive Christ and become born again. In fact, she may have needed deliverance before she could go on with her spiritual search. Not all power encounters result in dramatic salvations and deliverances. Usually, the hearts of others open more fully in response to Agape love expressed rather than to power released.

You Can Prepare for the Showdown

There are several prophets preparing Christians to move into the enemy's camp and release the presence and power of God in their midst. In a sense, they are raising up an army of young prophets (of varying chronologic ages). Doug Addison, Stacey Campbell, John Paul Jackson, and Patricia King have been forerunners in this move of God's heart to reach out to those engaged in occult activities. Many Charismatics and Pentecostals, who have experienced the empowering of the Holy Spirit to stand against the enemy of our souls, are being prepared to understand how to minister effectively and what it takes to infiltrate the ranks of modern-day Baal worshipers.

John Paul Jackson offers several keys to preparation for the coming showdown:

Every prophetic voice—from Moses to Daniel, from the apostle Paul to the church in Pergamos—has had to wrestle against the powers of darkness.

In a time when spiritual wickedness is accepted as the "norm," all aspects of the media are filled with the glamorization of demons, and witchcraft is being touted as funny and compassionate, the people of God need to shrewdly arise.

I have gone into and sent teams into the enemy's camp for years now. We have infiltrated New Age fairs; Burning Man; Mardi Gras; Haunted Happenings in Salem, Massachusetts; various film festivals; and other national and international gatherings too numerous to mention. As a result, we have seen salvation happen even in the darkest environments.

One day, we may well have a "showdown at the OK Coral" with the enemy, but today there are very few people of God who would dare step into the quagmire of this face-off. Simply put, most do not believe God would back them up. There are two encompassing reasons for this fear.

First, we have to ask ourselves how well we know God's ways. I have found that being gifted does not guarantee we actually know God's ways—the when, where, and why He does what He does. To walk in God's ways when confronting the dark powers in others, we need to start with five simple keys:

1. We must be spiritually clean before we can walk in God's power. To the degree we are not clean, the enemy has access to us.

2. We must be absolutely convinced that our God is God. To the degree we doubt the omnipotence, omniscience, and omnipresence of our God over their god, we give the enemy access to our lives.

3. We are to set the rules of engagement, not them. God's prophets never allowed the enemy to define the boundaries.

4. When we walk in His ways, God will move Heaven and earth on our behalf. Expect miracles to happen!

5. Last but not least, we must love others with the love that made Jesus known as the friend of sinners. Love is the match that kindles the flame, and people are quickly drawn to it.

The second reason for our fear of the enemy is that current church culture often programs Christians to stay away from those in the New Age, witchcraft, or any other cult such as Buddhism or Hinduism—they believe we will be contaminated or demonized simply by being among them. Sadly, this is tacit agreement that the one who is in them is greater than He who is in us. Scripture tells us the opposite, but do we really believe it? When the world of darkness and the world of light collide, there are five simple ways of knowing how ready we are for God's Spirit to flow through us.

1. We must know the authority of the power we have in God. Our God created all beings, even those that subsequently fell. By definition, the created can never be greater than that which created it.

2. We must understand that it is the Holy Spirit who has all the Father's power at His disposal. The Holy Spirit flowing through us changes those around us.

3. We must cultivate and live in the atmosphere of God's presence. Others will feel it when they are near us, and their spirits will long for it.

4. We must know the limitations of the powers of darkness, which are revealed in the ten plagues of Egypt.

5. We need to realize that to the degree the Spirit of God flows through us, others' abilities to use their demonically empowered gifts are impaired.

In conclusion, when interacting with those who do not know Jesus as their Savior, we need to remember that Jesus said, "It is kindness that leads to repentance." No one truly comes to the

Lord through obnoxious and aggressive behavior, but we have seen hundreds come to salvation through the expression of love, especially when it is mixed with the demonstration of God's power.[12]

Moving from Fear to Faith

Zephaniah 1 and the Book of Revelation speak of a time of darkness coming on the world, characterized by spiritual apostasy, natural and technological disasters, and increasing fear. Luke 11:33-36 also speaks of the light of God increasing in this darkness as the people of God become carriers of His light and presence into the world. Many prophets, as we have seen in this chapter, believe that those days are upon us now and will increase in intensity as we approach the close of the age.

If that is so, it becomes imperative that we as Christians draw so close to the Lord that we walk as carriers of His presence—releasing prophetic words, healing, encouragement, destiny, and miracles to those who are hungry to experience the incredible love and power of God in our day. It is equally imperative that we increase in faith and decrease in fear. Fear-based theology has nothing to offer the world.

We already know the end of the story of Elijah's and Jehu's confrontations with the prophets of Baal. Scripture also reveals the end of the story marking the close of this age. As Cooke wrote in the Foreword, we contend with the shadows of the world from a place of victory, not defeat:

"The showdown was over before it began. Elijah was not fighting to get victory. He was contending from the place of overcoming: the Presence of God. What God's people were witnessing was the power of God being expressed through the heart of a man who knew that His anointing came from his intimate relationship with the Lord.

Elijah couldn't lose. That's the significance of Mount Carmel."

And neither can we.

Endnotes

1. George Otis, *The Twilight Labyrinth,* (Grand Rapids, MI: Chosen Books, 1997), 258.

2. Ibid., 258.

3. This excerpt was written and contributed by Dr. Bill Hamon specifically for inclusion in this book. He is the author of several books including *Apostles, Prophets, and the Coming Moves of God.*

4. This excerpt was written and contributed by Jim Goll specifically for inclusion in this book.

5. Quotes and information about Mahesh Chavda cited in this chapter were derived from a telephone interview.

6. Based on a personal interview with John Sandford.

7. Joyner, *Prophetic Ministry*, 79.

8. Based on a telephone interview with Patricia King.

9. Based on a telephone interview with Stacey Campbell. For more information see www.revivalnow.com.

10. Based on a telephone interview with Doug Addison. For more information about his ministry see www.inlightconnection.com.

11. The team member was referred to me.

12. This excerpt was written and contributed by John Paul Jackson specifically for inclusion in this book.

CHAPTER 8

The Sound of Abundant Rain

The shadows of the day shifted into night as Elijah fought for the hearts of God's people. Finally, the occult powers defeated, it was time for the drought to break and Elijah listened intently, for the sound of the coming rain. Not long after the prophets of Baal lay dead on the battlefield, Elijah saw a cloud on the horizon, a tiny cloud the shape of a man's hand. But it was enough for him to hear the sound of the abundance of rain in that tiny cloud. The glory of God and the power of His Kingdom would soon turn from a scattering of raindrops to a downpour. The showdown with the prophets of Baal wasn't just a battle for the hearts of God's people. It was about the sound of the abundance of rain coming to shower down upon us all.

The downpour of Heaven's rain consumed the people. It was a shower of love that broke the drought and released them from the famine and dryness, as much a condition of the soil of their hearts as the soil of the earth they walked on.

The showdown captured the attention of God's people, now they faced the ultimate decision to follow God, to learn to hear His voice for themselves, and to usher in the coming King. Seven times Elijah sent his servant to stand at the edge of the mountain and peer out to sea, looking for the clouds herald-ing rain. The cloud would become a token of the heavens opening. (See 1 Kings 18:44-46.)

In a sense, the Charismatic church has stood on the mountaintops of past moves of God wondering if the clouds they see, the tokens of revival and re-newal, are the final rains spoken of in the Scriptures—the rains heralding the return of Christ and the close of this age. Every generation looks for open heavens, doors opening in Heaven, showers of blessings upon the people of God worldwide—not just isolated showers. And every generation sees them. However, during our present generation, tokens of miracles depicting open heavens are occurring throughout the world as never before. They are signs that make everyone wonder.

According to Bobby Conner, Baptist Pastor turned prophet and founder of Demonstration of God's Power ministry, "The biblical pattern is for the Church of Jesus Christ to be a powerful prophetic force in the world, not a puny, pathetic one. The Lord has sent us to do the same things with the same power that He did, as it says in Mark 16:20: *And they went forth, and preached every where, the Lord working with them, and confirming the word with signs fol-lowing.*"[1]

We are in for some manifestations of the Holy Spirit that will seem for-eign to many in the church. As a result, many will be tempted to speak against the manifest sense of God's presence. Many Christians reject what they do not understand or become jealous of others' experiences—especially when they see great power released through new Christians who have just walked in from the shadows and been hit with the light. Some will say that those manifestations came about as a result of occult power, or prophetic words as a result of divination. Others will reject them outright.

Still the fact remains, signs and wonders are breaking out all over the world. In the process, miracles of healing and power encounters are happen-ing not just to a select few in meetings, but overtaking the hundreds and thousands in attendance—en masse! Clouds of rain and glory, gold dust sparkling on people's hands and faces, angelic visitations, throne room expe-riences, and fourth dimension miracles—they are all signs appearing on the earth in the lives of individuals across the world. They are signs to make you wonder and listen for the sound of the abundance of rain, the heavens opening and a worldwide downpour of revelation and power that has not been seen ever before. It is a downpour that God is inviting you to experience.

The Abundance of Rain

In Imparatriz, Brazil, on September 8, 2005, former Vineyard pastor and Global Awakening Associate Minister Gary Oates stood preaching before a crowd of more than 3,000 people in the large Assemblies of God church. The church looked like a miniature football stadium with giant openings in the walls on several levels of the building to allow air flow. Not a cloud hovered in the starry night sky when we arrived at the church. Only the sliver of a new moon blinked its greeting from heaven giving no hint of what was in store. It was the dry season. Dust blew through the streets at will, piling up alongside the road and walls in houses topped with broken glass and barbed wire to keep out intruders. The city and the people were hot, thirsty, and afraid of each other.

Gary preached about Elijah, the sound of the abundance of rain, and about praying persistently for the rain of God's healing presence. Elijah, Gary explained, prayed seven times for rain, each time looking up to see if a cloud the size of a man's hand would sweep in and shower down an abundance of rain upon the people, breaking the drought. At the end of his story we heard the sound of the abundance of rain carried on the wind. Suddenly, a squall blew in through the windows, circulating rapidly counter-clockwise within the vast building. Palm trees bent and swayed ecstatically, dancing with the wind outside. The tangible presence of God swept through the church and the people rose to their feet cheering. Gary stood on the platform; his arms raised high overhead for about 10 minutes, as long as the rain and wind lasted.

God had completely suspended the laws of nature. Not only did rain come out of season and on a night of a new moon rather than a full moon as they had traditionally seen in the area, His Spirit Wind blew in as well. A woman stepped out from the pastor's office where a group of intercessors had gathered to pray. She and her family had been missionaries with New Tribes

157

mission in the area for more than 21 years. Just before dropping to her knees she said, "This never happens. This is a genuine miracle."

The rain continued pummeling the street but the palm trees finally stilled. Only a light wind blew outside. Eventually, it died down and the audience grew quiet, wondering. Oates invited people to receive the healing presence of the Lord, saying the Lord was present to heal. Indeed, He had just illustrated His message with signs and wonders. Hundreds of people received instant healings. Hundreds more received Jesus and entered into salvation that night. [2]

Signs To Make you Wonder — Glory Clouds and Gold

Mahesh Chavda stood before his congregation in Fort Mill, North Carolina, his Bible open to Second Corinthians 3:10 and read, *"For what was glorious has no glory now in comparison with the surpassing glory."* [3]

Nearly 1,000 people sat listening in the tent that serves as his sanctuary when something unusual drew their attention. Something was forming in the middle of the tent, emerging out of the empty air, taking shape, hovering just above the heads of several people. People started nudging one another, pointing to the unusual manifestation, wondering what it was. Within a few moments, Mahesh realized that he was losing his audience and looked up from the Word to see what drew their attention away.

A cloud had manifested in the middle of the tent shimmering with particles, feathers, dust that looked like gold. Hundreds of people started shouting out about the glory cloud. Others stood in total awe. It manifested stronger, beaming with light and glittery gold-like particles. The cloud stayed almost half an hour while Mahesh wagged his head with childlike delight, smiled, and started singing a simple chorus, "Where the Spirit of the Lord is there is liberty."

According to Mahesh, "It was quite inspiring and way beyond anything we had seen up to this point in our congregation or conferences. Other pastors who witnessed the glory cloud said it was the first time they had seen a manifestation of the presence of God like that. As it manifested, it released a great sense of love and honor for the Lord Jesus in our midst. We were so humbled."

Out-of-season squalls and clouds of glory appearing in churches seem strange enough to those who know they are witnessing something beyond their regional realm of experience. Another worldwide phenomenon has also captured the attention of thousands who have witnessed it. No one seems to know when and where the first reports of gold dust appearing on peoples' faces and hands during prayer and worship gatherings first started happening. There have been reports from all over the world for the past several years. The gold dust accounts are not confined to any one group, conference, or congregation of any particular size, nor are they attached to any one ministry or man. It seems as if the appearance of gold manifests on whomever the glory of God desires.

In 1997 Daryl Nicolet, pastor of Faith Worship Center in Pepperall, Massachusetts, and John Schweigert, pastor of Pilgrim Covenant Church at that time, were leading a small renewal service when manifestations of a glittery gold substance appeared on the people gathered. Nicolet had just read a few testimonies from the Toronto Airport Christian Fellowship about people suddenly and miraculously receiving gold fillings in their teeth and others seeing gold dust appear on hands and faces. Throughout the meeting, the presence of God grew stronger and many people were lying on the floor enjoying His presence. Around 11 P.M., Daryl looked at his fingers and noticed a glittery substance on his skin. "I am standing there looking at my fingers, just amazed because we had just read the testimonies. The glittery substance didn't seem to fall from the sky; it just seemed to come out of my pores and appear."[4]

He called his wife over and she too noticed the glitter of gold on his hands. Then she held up her own hands and realized that gold had appeared on her as well. Because of the late hour, many people had left the meeting to go home. About 44 people still remained. According to Nicolet, every single person remaining in the meeting had the substance on them. "No one prayed for them. There was no impartation prayer for this. It just was showing up on faces, arms, and elbows. Kids were running around smiling. They had it all over them. And it wasn't the make-up rage to wear glitter at the time. What was so amazing to me was that they all had it on them at the same time."

This appearance of gold dust, or "glory dust" as the Chavdas call it, has been sighted in South America, North America, Indonesia, Europe, and Africa during small meetings and large gatherings. In fact, some overseas reports indicate that small jewels, colored gem stones, have appeared in the hands of people while they were outstretched in worship. Believers speculate that the gold and jewels are signs of Heaven's opening, of God adorning His Bride (the Church), that occurs during moments of intimate individual and corporate worship.

Angelic Visitations and Feathers from Heaven

Over the past decade or so, reports of individuals seeing angels, talking with angels, and emphasizing that everyone can see them have dominated some segments of the Charismatic church. Individual and corporate encounters with unusual feathers falling in unusual times and places have also been reported. Manifestations of angels and feathers that materialize out of nowhere seem to be common occurrences, and are quite possibly authentic manifestations that are God-made rather than man-made. Some ministers stand in awe and wonder, refusing to let the manifestations detract from the focus on other aspects of the Kingdom, including the King. Other leaders feel a compulsion to interpret the meaning according to their own grid of understanding. The manifestation may be authentic; however, the interpretation may or may not. Still others, more immature ministers, use the manifestations to call attention to their ministries as if the manifestations are heavenly endorsements. These types of responses to manifestations both repel and attract people who want to know what is of God and what is not.

In a report written by Fresh Fire staff members, the ministry of young Canadian evangelist Todd Bentley, a number of manifestations of God were apparently seen by many during a conference held in British Columbia in 2005. With this current focus on the supernatural sweeping through Charismatic church circles, it provides a typical example of what people are reporting seeing in meetings worldwide—no matter who the main speaker or the size of the group. Bentley also explains why more manifestations show up in some places rather than others. His focus on supernatural power and manifestations has led many Christians to embrace increasing revelation and openness to greater dimensions of the Holy Spirit. Portions of the report follow:

> Feathers supernaturally appeared in the air and gently fell to the floor, as if God was opening up the Fresh Fire Ministries prophetic conference with a special divine sign of an open heaven over the place. This sign caught the attention of the capacity crowd at the Living in the Supernatural conference listening to the opening prophetic message of Revivalist and FFM founder Todd Bentley in Abbotsford, B.C., Canada. About 36 feathers seemed to appear in mid air, a few at a time, throughout the meeting—they started ten feet below the ceiling, before drifting to earth, as heaven invaded the building.

> In his opening message Todd referred to the appearance of feathers and an angel called Promise that had visited him just days before. He announced that God was releasing a new season in which promises given over the past 20 years would begin to come to pass. "There is something supernatural about this; I sense real divine destiny," he said. "There are actually angels in heaven that oversee answered prayer. They oversee what God has promised to be sure that it is released in your life, city and nation."

> In another session, Todd described some of the supernatural manifestations we can expect to see if we faithfully nurture our spiritual life by embracing kingdom thinking. He said that when we start to talk about "the stuff"—gold, angels, feathers, deliverance and healing—they show up! "Whatever you can expect to see in heaven eternally, should be what I can expect to see now in the spirit." Todd said that because there are so few supernatural experiences in the Church today, most believers do not expect them. "We settle for no supernatural experience because we want to play safe!" he said.

> "However, God has invited us to come boldly to His throne (a place of supernatural encounter). God has promised that He will pour out His Spirit on all flesh," continued Todd. "But you can't

speak the heart and mind of God if you aren't living in the super-natural and listening to His voice." Such a supernatural life in-volves trances, visions, dreams, angelic visitations, and being taken up into the third heaven. Todd examined Hebrews 6 in which Paul encourages believers to go on from the elementary principles (repentance, baptisms, laying on of hands, and basic doctrines) to the place of having *"tasted the good word of God and the powers of the age to come"* (v.5 NKJV). After we see into this realm of "the powers of the age to come," he said, we can decree what we see in order to bring them out of that realm into the natural realm.

Referring to Isaiah 2, 1 Corinthians 2, and Job 29, Todd noted that God wants to entrust His true friends with the kinds of revelation that Jesus experienced. He said we can have this revelatory wis-dom 24 hours a day. Then, just like Jesus, we will do nothing but what we see the Father doing.[5]

Third Heaven Experiences and Fourth Dimension Miracles

Scripture talks not only about doing what we see the Father doing, but of going beyond the works that Jesus did and doing "greater things." Ian Clay-ton, a prophet in New Zealand, believes these "greater things" include per-sonally experiencing the domain of the third heaven, which is the domain of God and fourth dimension miracles such as teleportations, walking through walls, and dematerializing in order to pass unharmed through a murderous crowd, walking on water, raising the dead, and performing miraculous works that transcend our natural laws of physics. Clayton is no stranger to the supernatural as revealed in Chapter 2. He has experienced many of the fourth-dimension miracles listed above, as have others, and regularly seeks to commune with God, not so much on earth, but in Heaven.

He believes that as sons and daughters of the King, we have a right to ex-plore the realm of Heaven and to walk back into the realms of earth bearing His presence, revelation and power. The realms of Heaven Clayton walks in include glimpses of the Garden in Eden, the throne room of God and areas of His Kingdom that few have seen and even fewer have words to describe.

Much of his ministry today focuses on revealing the inheritance Christians have as sons and daughters. He also brings people into the mystery of the supernatural, mentoring them along until people access the realms of Heaven for themselves and visionary experiences become super-Natural. Clayton believes anyone can be taught to access greater intimacy with Christ—literally on earth as it is in Heaven. And he stands in good company. Prophets Shawn Boltz and Patricia King have written about their experiences walking in the throne room of Heaven along with other revelatory ministers. John Sandford talks about his experiences involving accessing Heaven, the throne room, and entering into the council chambers of God. Clayton demystifies the experience by explaining that accessing Heaven can be a learned experience:

> Entering the realm of the Kingdom is a learned experience. The spirit-man can go with Jesus and walk with God because the Holy Spirit resides in your body. I surrender to the glory of God and then I walk with Him. He initiates it. I follow by my desire to be with the Father in His kingdom. As children we have a right to be with God the Father in Heaven. As a son He gives me a right to discover the realm of Heaven. My single desire is to encounter and know Him as a friend, to know all that He does and all that He is about. Every time I walk into the realms of Heaven, it always leads to a deeper love and encounter with God.[6]

Shifting Shadows of Supernatural Manifestations

While some believe the manifestations are authentic, others view the manifestations as metaphors—the gold and jewels as signs of financial provision coming, purity increasing, and the resources of Heaven being released for global evangelism. The glory clouds, rain squalls, and increasing angelic encounters are often interpreted as signs that Heaven is breaking forth into the earth today. Still others react in unbelief, considering the manifestations simply spiritualists' parlor tricks, concocted by charlatans to expand their reputations. A few believe that the signs that make people wonder are deceptions of the enemy—manifestations that are not from God.

John R.W. Stott, a British theologian, urges caution when trying to interpret the signs of the times and the manifestations of the Holy Spirit. According to Stott, "We all need, in these days in which the Holy Spirit seems to be stirring, to be sensitive to what he may be saying or doing among us. We must be very careful neither to blaspheme against the Holy Spirit by attributing his work to the devil, nor to quench the Holy Spirit by resolving to contain him within our own safe, traditional patterns."[7]

Pastor Bill Johnson, author of several books that catapult people into higher levels of faith resulting in an increase in supernatural signs and wonders, is a man stirring the nation to tap into their spiritual DNA and walk into the purposes of God for this generation. Yet he knows that spiritual manifestations frighten some people, others reject it for a variety of reasons.

According to Johnson, people reject what they don't understand. They feel uncomfortable and emphatically state it must not be from God. He speaks about the spirit of the antichrist at work attempting to reject anything that has to do with the Holy Spirit's anointing.

"Church leaders and individuals attempt to reject what they cannot control, to reduce the Gospel to an intellectual message rather than a supernatural God encounter, and fail to expect that God's power is available to everyone—right here and right now. The attitude of control erodes our faith until God's power is reduced to man's ability to reason.

"Every believer has written into his or her spiritual DNA the desire for the supernatural. It is our predetermined sense of destiny. This God-born passion dissipates when it has been taught or reasoned away, when it's not been exercised, or when it's been buried under disappointment."[8]

Many of those who have noticed their passion for God wane have also received a fresh surge of faith that dispels their unbelief during meetings where the presence of God manifests in unusual ways. Yet those who display antichrist attitudes that reject the Holy Spirit, a significant member of the Trinitarian God-head, are wide open to the commentators who seek to prey upon fear and release a measure of control. Calling themselves watchdogs over wrong theology, these commentators often turn the faith of many into fear—in direct violation of the very Scriptures they profess to protect.

As supernatural manifestations increase in the years to come we must take care to discern the shifting shadows of attitudes, soulish desires, and fears within us; leading us to interpret signs according to our own understanding. We must take care not to interpret the manifestations as Heaven's endorsements of any one minister or meeting. We must take care not to call evil "good" or good "evil." Finally, we must take care to stand in awe of God, not in awe of signs and wonders, and move in the nature of Christ expressing the marks of true power—namely, love and humility.

Watchdogs or Fear Mongrels

During Jonathan Edwards' times, the crowds were no different in their assessment of Charismatic phenomena. Edwards, a Congregational preacher and theologian, is known for launching the First Great Awakening, a revival that occurred in New England in the 1740s. He held meetings marked by tears and loud intercessions along with fainting and other "bodily effects", physical manifestations of the presence of God, as people came into an awareness of the state of their souls and their need of a Savior. After people left his meetings some reacted in faith, believing the conversions and manifestations of God's presence they witnessed were from God, while others reacted in fear and disbelief. Edwards' words of warning echo throughout the ages and serve to warn us still. "Let all to whom this work is a cloud and darkness…take heed that it not be their destruction while it gives light to God's Israel," Edwards said, referring to Acts 13:41 and scoffers who refuse to receive and speak contemptuously of the revival of God.[9]

He admonishes us not to confuse the shifting shadows of darkness and light and call good "evil" and evil "good." In Edwards' day, people aired their views in conversation and in print.

Today, self-appointed watchdogs proliferate and pontificate on the Internet, television, radio, and in books creating needless fears of deception. To be a cult watcher and keep tabs on demonic activity in the world is one thing. But Edwards, an ardent Calvinist and dispensationalist in the early days of his ministry, admonished Christians that it was quite another to sit in judgment over brothers and sisters in Christ and to presume to sit in judgment over God.

One of the marks of God's true power and authority is the ability to move in love—not to be motivated by their own over-inflated egos and call attention to their "wisdom."

Another mark of God's power is humility—not arrogance but a willingness to learn from others rather than stand apart and judge others. Perhaps most importantly, one of the greatest marks of God's power and authority is to stir up a passion to enter into the fullness of God—knowing God's love, His power, and His purpose, drawing others into deeper relationship with God and greater commitment to fulfilling their destinies.

According to these characteristics of one who moves in the true power of God, watchdogs, apparently, do not fit the description of true power brokers of the Word. In fact, M. Scott Peck, a noted psychiatrist, points out the pathology and error driving the personalities of these watchdogs and scoffers—drawing a connection between the person and spirit whispering in their ears. He writes, "Evil people and spirits are both characterized by a kind of excessive pride or narcissism that causes them to believe they are without fault. Satan is renowned for speaking the truth in one sentence while lying in the next." [10]

Those who feel like they need to maintain a grip on their ministry or their seat of authority by seeking to discredit the ministries of others should heed the words of a wise man:

> "...let them alone; for if this plan or this undertaking is of men, it will fail; but if it is of God, you will not be able to overthrow them. You might even be found opposing God!" [11]

We have no need to fear deception.

Why do people listen to fear mongers? Counselors have a saying that "the issue isn't really the issue." Fear of deception isn't really the issue for many people; fear of change is a greater issue on their hearts.

Fear of change is one of the biggest hindrances to personal growth. Stretching your belief system, changing the way you think requires a corresponding shift in behavior and action. Behavioral change follows cognitive change. When people are confronted with new ideas about God, they must either incorporate those ideas into their belief system or reject them. Once accepted, a whole chain reaction occurs that continually nudges people out of their comfort zones.

For instance, if a person doesn't believe that God speaks personally then encounters God in a personal way—through a dream or through someone giving them a prophetic word—they must make a decision to accept or reject this new idea about the nature of God. If accepted, then they are responsible to seek a deeper relationship with God. Once open to greater revelation from God, they are then confronted with the possibility that God may say something they don't like and they will be called to take some action that was not in their game plan. That action may be something like repent, change your actions, forgive, or learn to let go of your anger toward another. Or it may be something more dramatic such as a calling to ministry or to another place.

However, if the person rejects the dream or the prophetic word, then there seems to be no reason to take personal responsibility to stretch your thinking or respond to whatever God says about what may follow. Repeated clashes of beliefs may only result in anger and frustration rather than openness to a deeper, personal relationship with a loving God.

For those who are impacted by the words of these watchdogs it is time to step out of the shadows of fear and into the light of God's presence. As Johnson says, "What do I trust most, my ability to be deceived or His ability to keep me? And why do you think He gave us the Comforter? He knew His ways would make us uncomfortable first." [12]

The Power and the Presence

According to Bobby Conner, the manifestations of God's presence and increasing signs of open heavens are bringing the Church to the point of discovering the real issue at stake—that of yielding our life completely to the purposes of the Holy Spirit. Conner explains:

> The real issue is not whether or not we want the power of God, but do we really want the presence of God in our lives? God is seeking to build character in us, the character of His Son! This is

not *instead* of His power, but *because* of His power. The anointing of the Holy Spirit is not just a one time touch; it is a transformed life, a life that is yielded daily to the Holy Spirit's control. As the apostle said in Galatians 2:20:

I am crucified with Christ: nevertheless I live; yet not I, but Christ liveth in me: and the life which I now live in the flesh I live by the faith of the Son of God, who loved me, and gave himself for me. (KJV)

This is our calling, that we not live only for ourselves, but that the Lord might live His life through us. Moses knew the only thing that would make us different and unique from anyone else in the world would be the manifest presence of God revealed in our midst, as he stated in Exodus 33:14-16:

And He said, "My presence shall go with thee, and I will give thee rest." And he (Moses) said unto Him, "If Thy presence go not with me, carry us not up hence. For wherein shall it be known here that I and Thy people have found grace in thy sight? Is it not in that thou goest with us? So shall we be separated, I and Thy people, from all the people that are upon the face of the earth." (KJV)

It is not just knowing about Jesus, but having Him present with us that is essential. The presence of the Lord is not an occasional touch from Him, with which so many Christians become satisfied. It is the presence and power of Almighty God in our daily lives—it is a continual filling of the Holy Spirit so that we abide in Him each day. This is the only way that true Christians can be distinguished from all of the other religions on the face of the earth. Christianity is not just knowing or trying to live by certain doctrines—it is becoming the temple of the Holy Spirit.

This reality is revealed again in the example of Peter and John standing before the council in Acts 4:13:

Now when they saw the boldness of Peter and John, and perceived that they were unlearned and ignorant men, they marveled; and they took knowledge of them, that they had been with Jesus.

168

It was not Peter's and John's intellectual ability that caught the attention of these men—it was the fact that they had been with Jesus. There is a noticeable quality in those who have been in fellowship with the Lord.[13]

In addition to tangible signs of God's world breaking into ours—through dreams, visions, angelic appearances, glory clouds, nature miracles, gold dust and gems suddenly appearing, and others—there is one manifestation that seems timeless and undeniable to all who feel it. It is the manifestation of the presence of God, overwhelming in love, peace, joy, that comes like a smothering kiss causing the beloved to swoon and fall or laugh and dance with joy. It is this sign and wonder that inflames the passion for Christ and His Kingdom come, more than any other.

Matt Sorger, a prophetic minister based in New York, wrote about this phenomenon of presence experienced during a conference held in Long Island, New York in 2005. It is a phenomenon that has been experienced all over the world in decades past as well as in our day. Sorger writes:

> What a powerful weekend we had during our 3rd regional Healing in His Wings Signs and Wonders Conference in Long Island, NY. There was a great sense of unity, expectation and spiritual hunger as over 21 churches gathered together from across the New York region and beyond to experience a fresh touch from the Holy Spirit. Many were filled, refreshed, healed, delivered, and empowered to live in a place of overcoming victory in their walk with God. Each night God moved in a unique and powerful way as His Glory swept over His people.
>
> As I entered the sanctuary Saturday night a man came running up to me with tears in his eyes proclaiming how wonderful God's presence was in the church. The air was electrified with God's glory and everyone could feel Him there. It wasn't just another meeting. It was a night of holy encounter. As we lifted up our hearts in worship to God people could be seen weeping as their

hearts were touched in a profound and unusual way by the Holy Spirit, some for the very first time.

On Sunday night during our anointing service the glory of God swept into the room in a corporate way. There are those times when the entire room becomes filled with the manifest glory of God, which is what we pray and long for in our meetings. It wasn't church as usual. A true revival spirit was released among us. Many began to burn with the tangible fire of God. As God's glory broke in people were "blown back" by the power all around the room. A wave of "holy laughter" broke out as people were filled and refreshed by the glory of God. The atmosphere of heaven invaded the lives of those present. [14]

When the church experiences the manifest presence of God, the power is undeniable. The shifting shadows of doubt and unbelief are blown away by the kiss of God. Healing and deliverance comes as a natural byproduct during meetings such as the one Sorger described. The presence releases a revelatory atmosphere of Heaven that often imparts to individuals a sense of calling and personal destiny, visions of things to come, angelic visitations, and experiences of the revelatory realms of Heaven. It is this sense of God's presence that delights the senses more than external manifestations of gold, glory clouds, and others signs that make people wonder.

No one who has experienced such intimacy of encounter with the tangible, sensory awareness of the presence of God can deny that He exists and that He is the God who is love. All other gods pale in comparison to Him. All other shadows flee. When His presence manifests more fully, no one will be lost in darkness.

Endnotes

1. Excerpted from the article, "The Power of God," by Bobby Conner and posted on his Website at www.bobbyconner.com. Bobby Connor

has a ministry called *A Demonstration of God's Power*, in Moravian Falls, North Carolina.

2. Based on personal observation. I was the team member who witnessed the nature miracle and talked with the missionary. Gary Oates, former pastor currently working as an itinerant minister and associate of Randy Clark's ministry, is the author of *Open My Eyes, Lord—A Practical Guide to Angelic Visitations and Heavenly Experiences* (Dallas, GA: Open Heaven Publications, 2004). See www.garyoates.com.

3. Based on a telephone interview with Mahesh Chavda.

4. Quotes and information about Daryl Nicolet cited in this chapter are based on a personal interview.

5. Excerpted from the article, "Supernatural Signs Appear at Prophetic Conference," a Fresh Fire Ministries Conference Report written by staff members. Posted April 28, 2005, at www.elijahlist.com.

6. Based on a telephone interview with Ian Clayton.

7. John R.W. Stott, *The Baptism and Fullness of the Holy Spirit.* (London: Inter-Varsity Fellowship, 1964), 57-60.

8. Johnson, *When Heaven Invades Earth*, 81.

9. Randy Clark, *Lighting Fires.* (Lake Mary, FL: Charisma House, 1998), 111.

10. M. Scott Peck, *Glimpses of the Devil: A Psychiatrist's Personal Accounts of Possession, Exorcism and Redemption.* (New York: Free Press, Simon & Schuster, Inc., 2005), 180.

11. Acts 5:38-39 ESV.

12. Johnson, *When Heaven Invades Earth*, 83.

13. Conner, "The Power of God."

14. Excerpted from original posting on Matt Sorger's Website at www.mattsorger.com.

PART THREE

CHAPTER 9

You Can Access Supernatural Power

In this present world of spiritual darkness and shifting shadows of supernatural power, Christians everywhere are being confronted with several important questions. They are questions that you must answer for yourself before you seek to access greater authority, revelatory visions, prophetic insights, and supernatural power:

Why do I want to experience an increase of supernatural power in my life?

Are there shifting shadows of loyalty in my heart evidenced through my behaviors and actions?

Am I experiencing God's manifest presence and so captivated by God's love that my life overflows with the radiant presence of God?

How willing am I to embrace the cross of Christ?

What must I do to prepare for an increase in power and authority to take victory over the shifting shadows of darkness in my given sphere of influence at work and at home?

Why Do You Want More Power?

Signs, miraculous healings, revelatory and prophetic insights are amazing gifts that testify of Jesus. They do not endorse an individual's ministry.

Neither do they validate an individual or a movement as being blessed or favored by the Father. Signs and wonders do not validate truth and they will not validate who you are. So why do you want the power of God moving through your life?

During a series of talks with his staff members, the late Derek Prince, a man who moved in revelatory power, signs and wonders, expressed his concern about today's emphasis on Christians moving in power.

Through his decades of ministry he had seen the excesses and abuses of power. He had also watched how people could move under the anointing of two different spirits—the Holy Spirit's anointing and the anointing of a demonic spirit. In various works, Prince cites the biblical example of King Saul and the case of William Branham's healing ministry as examples of men who operated in two different spirits. Prince's caution is both sobering and enlightening:

> I find today in our contemporary church, if you preach about power, everybody gets excited—and if you appeal for people who want to receive power, many will come forward. Personally, I believe this emphasis on power can be extremely dangerous. I have observed over a good many years that people who focus on power end in trouble. They often end in error.

> Power is something that appeals to the natural man. Some psychologists have said that the desire for power is the number one desire of the human personality. Paul said, "I want power, but I want it on a different basis from that which the world understands. I want to forget all my wisdom, all my knowledge, all my theological qualifications and I want to focus on only one thing: Jesus Christ crucified." [See 1 Corinthians 2:1-5.] And then he said, in effect, "When I do that, I can be sure that the Holy Spirit will come in power." [1]

Prince encourages believers to know the Word of God, embrace the cross of Christ, and dwell in His glory—not seeking our own. Having a love for the truth, knowing the Word of God, and seeking to remain in His presence, will keep many from being deceived by spirits that imitate the power of the Holy Spirit.

Now, the Bible speaks about signs and wonders. It says some things about them that are good, and some that are very frightening. I want to turn to 2 Thessalonians chapter 2 and read a few verses there, beginning at verse 9.

The coming of the lawless one [that is the title of the antichrist] is according to the working of satan, with all power, signs, and lying wonders, and with all unrighteous deception among those who perish, because they did not receive the love of the truth, that they might be saved. And for this reason God will send them strong delusion, that they should believe the lie, that they all may be condemned who did not believe the truth but had pleasure in unrighteousness (2 Thess. 2:9-12).

So, Paul says here there are such things as lying signs and wonders. There are true signs and there are lying signs. True signs attest the truth. Lying signs attest lies. Satan is fully capable of supernatural signs and wonders. Unfortunately, many in the Charismatic movement have the attitude that if something is supernatural, it must be from God. There is no scriptural basis for that assumption. Satan is perfectly capable of producing powerful signs and wonders to attest his lies, and the reason such people are deceived is *because they did not receive the love of the truth*. On such people God will send *strong delusion*.

That is one of the most frightening statements in the Bible. If God sends you *strong delusion*, you will be deluded. I think that is one of the most severe judgments of God recorded in Scripture, sending these people *strong delusion*. They will be condemned, these people, because *they did not believe the truth but had pleasure in unrighteousness*.

Therefore, signs and wonders are not a guarantee that something is the truth. There is only one sure way to know the truth. It is in the Word of God. Jesus said in John 8:32, *"You shall know the truth, and the truth shall make you free."* (NKJV) There is no other way to be sure that we can escape deception in these days except that we know and apply the truth of God's Word, the Scripture.

Are There Shifting Shadows of Loyalty in Your Heart?

Are you living in a house of shifting shadows? If so, are you willing to let the light of God penetrate your heart, releasing healing and deliverance to you?

In the opening chapter of this book, the shifting shadows of the house that the family had moved into brought them all into contact with great power and richly tragic spiritual experiences. Their dabbling in the occult—reading about spiritualism, taking mind-expanding drugs, contact with mediums and tarot cards, flirting with the devil, playing with white magic and casting spells, attempting astral travel, and willingly praying for spirit guides to come in and take them on spiritual adventures—lead to oppression in every area of their lives. Even today, many Christians are straddling both sides of the fence—seeking personal prophesies from Christian prophets, astrological forecasts, and psychics. The resulting oppression leads to spiritual destruction.

If you are dabbling in the occult, you need to renounce your reliance on demonic revelation and invite the Lord to release you from the resulting oppression. If you are seeking others to hear the voice of God for yourself, stop. The Lord loves you, too. And He wants to speak with you directly. Open the Word of God and start reading until His voice leaps off the page and releases the revelation of the Word into your ear and heart.

Even if you are not in overt rebellion or seeking demonic power, how much of God's light and love do you allow into your heart, mind, and soul? Of the two girls who walked out of the dark lord's shadow lands at the beginning of the book, Tami stopped at the edge of intimacy with Jesus. She received a measure of the Lord's healing embrace but shied away from the radiance of His ongoing presence of love and light. She built her house in a grey place, the realm that Graham Cooke, in the foreword of this book, calls "the shifting shadows of loyalty which people can inhabit when they do not reside in the light, close to the beacon of faithfulness." Ann, however, chose to live in the center of light captivated by the radiance of God's smile, her reality shaped by intimacy with Christ, her life a testimony of the power of the Holy Spirit.

There is no shadow of turning in Christ Jesus. If you are not basking in His light, you are being impacted by the shadows. If you are not abandoning yourself to Christ daily, who are you giving yourself to?

Does Your Life Overflow With the Radiant Presence of God?

The more the light of God's love consumes us the more effortlessly we extend that light, that atmosphere of Heaven, to the dark lord's kingdom. Do you bask in the light of God's presence? Do you adore intimacy with God? Do you only hear the commands of God or can you see His smile? Does the radiance of God shine through your life? There is so much more of His presence to experience, as well as His power.

The challenge of increasing in supernatural power is not to seek to move in power but to move in the presence of God. Rather than praying, "More Power!" cry out, "More of you, Lord!" That prayer enlarges your spirit and increases your spiritual sensitivity to hear the voice of God and act on the revelation that He releases to you. The overflow of His presence is supernatural power. The overflow of your presence is merely an expression of soulish power that is most likely tapping into second heaven revelation…the realm of demonic revelation. Do you want God's power or do you want Him? You can release the gifts of the Spirit; however, God cannot and will not be used. God desires intimate relationship with you, not overt manipulation.

The more we abandon ourselves to Him, the less we stumble around in the shifting shadows of loyalty and the more we release the manifest presence of God wherever we go. Then, what the world will witness is the power of God being expressed through the hearts of men and women who know their anointing comes from a deep, intimate relationship with the Lord. As more individuals and groups of believers grow in faith, we will see a convergence of supernatural power and intimacy. Believers will release not only a sense of God's presence in their homes, workplaces and in the world, but will discover that they have become super-Natural power brokers as well, imbued with gifts of healing, prophetic and revelatory insights, and miracles.

Are You Willing to Embrace the Cross of Christ?

Christ's death and resurrection is central to Christianity. It is the foundation of our love for others and our love for God. That resurrection power is available to all of us today—for salvation, healing, deliverance, and empowerment for ministry. The power of the Cross, the power of the redemptive blood of Jesus, is the greatest recurring sign and wonder in the earth today.

According to Prince, understanding and focusing on the Cross, on Christ crucified, will release a purity of revelation and power:

> In Matthew 16:24-25 Jesus says: *If anyone desires to come after Me, let him deny himself, and take up his cross, and follow Me. For whoever desires to save his life* [literally, soul] *will lose it, but whoever loses his life* [literally, soul] *for My sake will find it.* (NKJV)

> Here is the divine paradox: to save (protect) our soul we must lose it. Before we can follow Jesus, there are two preliminary steps. First, we must deny ourselves; we must say a resolute and final "No!" to our demanding, self-seeking ego. Second, we must take up our cross. We must accept the sentence of death which the cross imposes on us. Taking up our cross is a voluntary decision that each of us must make. God does not forcefully impose the cross upon us.

> If we do not apply the cross personally in our own life, we leave a door open to demonic influence. There is always the danger that our uncrucified ego will respond to the seductive flatteries of deceiving demons. Pride is the main area in our character which satan targets and flattery is the main lever he uses to gain entrance.

> We must each apply the Cross personally to ourselves. In Galatians 2:20 Paul says, *I have been crucified with Christ; it is no longer I who live...* (NKJV). We each need to ask: Is that true of me? Have I really been crucified with Christ? Or am I still motivated by my soulish ego?

> I believe one of our greatest needs is to focus on the Cross. I have seen people become very ambitious, striving for success, wanting

to build a large church or ministry. Sometimes they succeed, but unless the whole message is focused on the Cross, they have only wood, hay, and straw.

Embracing the Cross involves a willingness to die to selfish ambition, to wield the power of God for the sake of others and for the glory of the Lord. Embracing the Cross also means embracing the willingness to suffer for the sake of the Gospel. If your desire is to minister in power for your sake, to glorify self, that pride will lead to destruction. If your desire is to walk more intimately with God, doing what you see the Father doing, glorifying Him, then you will be able to endure the Cross—discovering victory in suffering that comes with ministering in power and enduring the agony of temporal defeat.

Part of the reason people shy away from moving in miraculous power and divine healing is because of the agony of defeat many Christians suffer after praying for individuals to be healed and seeing them carried away unchanged. The grief causes many people to be turned off by the healing movement and walk away from praying bold prayers for healing. Defeat, facing the suffering of others and suffering the heartache of ministering to others is part of embracing the cross of Christ who endured all things and triumphed over them.

According to Randy Clark, most people who believe that Jesus heals today but don't pray for healing fail to pray because they won't embrace suffering.

"Following the Lord involves a willingness to join in His suffering. Taking up your cross involves suffering. At the very least there is an emotional price tag that involves disappointment when people are not healed and personal challenges in family life and finances as you rearrange your life to follow the Lord.

If you are to prepare for an increase in power, you must understand that walking in the power of the Holy Spirit involves suffering and a continual humbling process. Not everyone you pray for

181

will be healed. Your heart will ache over those who are desperate for a touch from God and don't receive the miracle they seek."[2]

How Can You Prepare for an Increase in Power and Authority?

This last question can best be answered by those international ministry veterans who have witnessed signs and wonders accompanying their ministries. Making a conscious choice to learn from those whose ministries are characterized by Richard Foster's seven marks of power that come from God (referred to in the first chapter) will launch you into greater measures of faith and anointing. Here is how you can recognize those who can help you increase in power and authority. They may or may not have national or international recognition; yet their lives and ministries are characterized by:

- Power motivated by love and compassion to release salvation, deliverance, and healing;
- Power expressed with humility, deferring to one another's gifts, willing to learn from others, aware that the gifts flow from God as He wills;
- Power expressed with restraint, not under compulsion to the needs and distractions of men or the desire to express flashy revelation or miracles that draw attention to them;
- Power expressed with joy, operating from a basis of rest rather than exhaustion which can lead to delusion, filled with the presence of the Lord;
- Power that does not dominate or control but is revealed in vulnerability rather than bravado;
- Power that is submitted in right relationship to the Lord Jesus Christ and to others;
- Power that freely gives and sets people free rather than binding them in some obligation (financial or emotional) to the minister or ministry.

Healing evangelist Randy Clark is one of the international ministry veterans whose ministry expresses the seven marks of power that come from God. According to Clark:

> You sustain the move of God in your life and in the Church the same way you prepare for it—by simply praying, *God I want your*

power. But you don't just pray for power. *You must also pray, God I want your heart, your love for the poor, the broken and sick. I want to be able to stand in line for hours and pray and enjoy it.* Ministry is not about a power kick. It's about entering into the heart of God and feeling His love for the people. That's what sustains you for hours and hours of ministry. It's the love of God and obedience to the call.

Two other internationally known ministers, whose ministries express the seven marks of power that come from God—Mahesh Chavda and Bill Johnson—offer their wisdom in the final chapters of this book. Let them encourage you to embrace your spiritual destiny and inheritance and increase in super-Natural revelation and power. Read on and let their wisdom motivate you to embrace the Cross and increase in both power and authority for the glory of God.

I leave you with this final question: In the coming days, when the showdown between the "prophets of Baal" and the true prophets of God emerges more dramatically in the Church and the world, whose power will be seen as greater—God's or satan's? The answer lies within you.

ENDNOTES

1. All quotes in this chapter are based on a series of talks given by Derek Prince to his coworkers. The original recording of the series, "Protection from Deception," is available through Derek Prince ministries in March 1996. See www.derekprince.com.

2. All quotes in this chapter are based on a September 2005 interview with Randy Clark.

CHAPTER 10

Preparing for an Increase of Power

BY BILL JOHNSON

Jesus had no supernatural capabilities in Himself. Everything He did, He did as a man, completely dependant on the Holy Spirit. He emphasized this point by saying, *"The Son can do nothing of Himself."* [1]

While He is 100 percent God, He chose to live with the same limitations and restrictions that man would face once he was redeemed. He made that point over and over again. If He performed miracles as God, I am still impressed, but not compelled to follow. His example would be admirable, but unattainable. Yet it is obvious that He intended His disciples to do all that He did, and more. [2] Realizing that He did all the miracles as a man, I am responsible to follow the example He established, and pursue the spiritual realms He said were available to me. [3] By doing it this way He became a model for all who would become His disciples, thus embracing the invitation to invade the impossible in His name. He performed miracles, signs, and wonders, as a man in right relationship to God...not as God. Recapturing this simple truth changes everything...and makes possible a full restoration of the ministry of Jesus Christ in His Church.

Mission Impossible

To fulfill His mission, Jesus needed the Holy Spirit; and that mission, with all its objectives, was to finish the Father's work. If the Son of God was that reliant upon the anointing of the Holy Spirit, His behavior should clarify our need for the Holy Spirit's power upon us to do what the Father has assigned. We must be clothed with the Holy Spirit for supernatural ministry.

Part of our problem is this: we are accustomed to do only the things that are not impossible. If God does not show up and help us with most of our endeavors, we can still succeed. There must be an aspect of the Christian life that is impossible without divine intervention. That keeps us on the edge and puts us in contact with our true calling. It is our privilege to declare who He is by our obedient invasion into that which cannot be done without God's power being displayed.

Such a display of power was a core value of the early church. So great was the disciple's need for power to become witnesses that they were not allowed to leave Jerusalem until they had experienced what the Father had promised.[4] This power came to ordinary people who walked in intimacy with Jesus—through an experience with God called the Baptism in the Holy Spirit.[5] That encounter was not to be a one-time event, but was supposed to be an ongoing priority in the Christian life.[6]

The Importance of Experience

One of the tragedies we experience in this day is that great truths have been reduced to doctrines, and are avoided as experiences.[7] Near the top of the list is the wonderful declaration that we are seated *"in heavenly places in Christ."*[8] It has come to be a comforting promise for those who have problems, instead of a revelation of something that is available in Christ to all who believe. It is to be a third heaven experience that gives us a perspective on reality that no doctrine can accomplish by itself. This is very instrumental in learning to see things from God's perspective. Out of that place of intimacy we are uniquely positioned for purpose. And all who taste of this reality begin living from Heaven toward earth.

If the Holy Spirit is free to move more powerfully in our lives, we will constantly be involved in the invasion of impossibilities. The supernatural is His natural realm. The more important the Holy Spirit becomes to us, the less we will quench[9] and grieve[10] Him. Our desire will be to move in the supernatural to accomplish the purposes that God has created for us.

To prepare ourselves for an increase of power, we must answer this central question: How dependent on the Holy Spirit are we willing to be?

The Power and the Purpose

We believe it's our commission to change the world and alter the course of human history. Jesus said, *"...he who believes in Me, the works that I do he will do also; and greater works than these he will do, because I go to my Father"* (John 14:12). Jesus' prophecy of us doing greater works than He did has stirred the Church to look for some other meaning to this very simple statement. Many theologians seek to honor the works of Jesus as unattainable, which is religion[11] fathered by unbelief. Jesus showed us what one person could do who has the Spirit without measure. What could millions do? That was His point, and it became His prophecy.

Someone's got to catch His dream. Someone's got to hear what is possible through those dreams. We've got to think in terms of nations coming to God, and a nation coming in a day. God has been prophesying of a generation coming into the works of God where the weakest among us will be like David and the strongest like God.[12] Our assignment is to invade the impossible all over the world.

The purpose of Kingdom power is to invade society at its greatest places of need. Jesus said the Gospel of the Kingdom would be preached all over the world before the end comes. Most every time He uses the word *kingdom*, it is to display power. When power is demonstrated, people are released from torment, healed from their diseases, and are exposed to miracles of all sorts. If we carry that message with those results we know we are doing the same thing as Jesus.

Kingdom thinking knows that anything is possible at any time. It's activated when you and I with tender hearts surrender to the thought patterns of

God. It's when we receive His imaginations and say "yes" that we are changed. The Bible calls this the renewed mind. We know our minds are renewed when the impossible looks logical. We want our minds to be full of the leaven of the Kingdom[13]—living under Kingdom influence. We want miracles to have their full effect in us, changing the way we see and behave.

This is not just for those whose ministry is primarily within the confines of a church building or organization. Kingdom thinking impacts every realm of society—the businessman, the educator, and the politician alike. The King then influences how things should be done, revealing new ways of impacting people in our given spheres of influence. It is time to take the realms of influence back and impact secular society with the good news of God's Kingdom. Remember, the world only has a voice where the Church is silent. And without His message of the Kingdom, we have little to say.

Jesus is the *"desire of all nations."*[14] They just don't know it. Everyone seems to be seeking for a city whose builder and maker is God[15], they just don't realize they're crying out for the King and His rule. That's where we step into the picture. And that's where we come in displaying His love and power, re-presenting Him accurately.

Receiving and Releasing Our Inheritance

Because the concept of spiritual inheritance has been lost or ignored for decades, we have been working without the spiritual wealth previous generations have stored up for our use in these last days. Learning how to receive our inheritance and live from the accomplishments of prior generations will be key for us to succeed in our purpose in this hour.

The last 2,000 years of history show us that a revival will typically come and last two to four years, then fade out. Because of this pattern, an entire branch of theology has developed that says revival is supposed to arrive periodically to give the Church a shot in the arm—new enthusiasm, new hunger, new energy. But by saying that revival is an exception, normal Christianity is dumbed down to its lowest level. Revival is not an exception. Revival is the norm. Signs, wonders, and miracles are as normal to the Gospel as it is normal for you to get up in the morning and breathe. Revival is the Christian life. You cannot separate the two. We were never intended to live a season of life outside the outpouring of the Spirit of God. He always takes us from *"glory to glory."* [16] He is progressive in every move He makes. The nature of His kingdom is this: *"of the increase of His government and peace there will be no end."* [17]

The tragedy of human history is that revival comes and goes without continuous advancement. Subsequent generations build monuments around the achievements of the previous generation, but do not completely receive and occupy their inherited spiritual territory. We've never seen it increase in momentum from one generation to the next. Perhaps they don't want to pay the same price their forefathers paid. Or it's possible that some get distracted by forming organizations around the accomplishments of past movements. But preservation is not revival. Revival is a fire that either advances or dies. In either case, we inherit territory for free, but do not pay the price for expansion. In the Kingdom, inherited territory must be advanced or we lose it. Ask the man who received one talent. He thought that it was okay to preserve what he was given by his master. But He ended up losing the very thing he preserved. [18] This Kingdom only knows expansion!

Let me illustrate this point. Show me a church or a family whose forefathers broke into significant signs and wonders in the realm of healing, and I can show you descendents who were heavily afflicted with disease if they didn't maintain and expand their area of inherited breakthrough. The enemy waits for the opportunity to move into unoccupied territory once possessed by our forefathers. When the victories of past generations go unoccupied, they become the platform from which the enemy mocks the victories of the past generation. Worse yet, that unoccupied territory becomes the military encampment from which the enemy launches an assault against the people of God to erase from their memories their inherited victories. When we back off of the standard that God has set, we literally invite the devourer to destroy.

Instead of building on the foundations laid by the likes of John Lake, Smith Wigglesworth, and Aimee Semple McPherson, we build memorials to their accomplishments, and forget what we should have inherited. And once again, we have to re-dig a well, remove the humanistic, rationalistic approach to life that denies the Creator Himself and His purpose in creating man as delegated authority over a planet. These elementary principles must be fully embraced and built upon for the generations ahead to experience things we never thought possible.

Fatherless Revivalists

Every generation of revivalists has been fatherless as it pertains to a move of the Spirit. Every generation has had to learn from scratch how to recognize the presence, how to move with Him, and how to pay a price. The answer to this dilemma is found in recovering our spiritual inheritance.

An inheritance is receiving something that someone else paid a price for. And if we're going to leave something to those who follow us, we'll have to pay a price to expand what we got for free.

God is serious about returning for a glorious church. He's serious about nations serving Him—not just a token representation from every tribe and tongue, but entire nations, entire people groups apprehended by God Himself. We were never intended to start over from scratch every two or three generations. God wants to put each generation at a higher level than the previous. We dishonor our forefathers and the great price they paid to get their breakthrough by not showing genuine honor for what they accomplished by giving ourselves to expansion and increase.

How do we receive this spiritual inheritance? Honor. When children honor their parents, they are promised long life. Life is released in honor. When we honor a prophet in the name of a prophet, we receive the prophet's reward. Prophets pay a tremendous price to walk in their gift. But honor is valued so highly in Heaven that you step into their reward simply through honor. This wonderful tool gives us access to the lost mantles of the past. Through honor we can tap into the grace that our heroes of former days lived in. What we receive in our inheritance will be equal to the honor we give.

We must ask the Lord for an increase in wisdom to understand what that inheritance looks like in us as individuals and as a corporate body of believers. His anointing will lead us to receive all that He has for us and more—leading us into new territories. This is how we move into new territory, by building on precept after precept. Truth is progressive and multi-dimensional. It constantly evolves as we grow, though it never evolves into something that contradicts its foundations. There are measures and levels of anointing that cause the reality of the Scripture to change for us.

A generation is forming now that will walk in an anointing that has never been known by mankind, including the original 12 disciples. This generation won't need natural illustrations to help them understand what their spiritual task is. They will move into spiritual territory that defies the natural order. God wants to give us revelations and experiences of Heaven that have no earthly parallel. Jesus told Nicodemus, *"If I have told you earthly things and you do not believe, how will you believe if I tell you heavenly things?"* (John 3:12) He longed to talk about things that His disciples were not ready to receive.

Beyond Measure

Jesus walked in an anointing of the Spirit beyond measure. He constantly illustrated superior truths by stepping outside the boundaries of nature. The more you and I become empowered and directed by the Spirit of God, the more our lives should defy natural principles, and release the spiritual realities God intended for us to enjoy.

We are in the beginning stages of the season of accelerated growth. I believe it is possible, under the mercy of God, to make up for several hundred years of failure in these areas. It's possible to lay the groundwork for another generation to come and use our ceiling as their floor, to build upon it, and go where no one has ever gone.

First Corinthians 12-14 contains wonderful teaching on the operation of the gifts of the Spirit. But beyond that it is a revelation of the body of believers who live in the realm of the Spirit that is essential for an authentic gospel. These manifestations of the Holy Spirit are being taken to the streets where they belong. It is there that they reach their full potential. Our ambition is to increasingly take that atmosphere of Heaven wherever we go, whether it's into our homes, businesses, the streets, or the even the mall. This is the normal Christian life.

In the city where I live, community members are recognizing the impact believers are having as they take the power of God to the streets. People are accepting Christ into their lives, being instantly healed and delivered. The Kingdom of God is advancing through signs, wonders, healings, and power encounters. Hundreds of people have been healed in public places through believers that believe God is good.

We are living in desperate times. Genuine hunger accelerates the process of maturity. And truly desperate people can pull into this hour what was reserved for another hour.

A New Day of Power

This generation has the opportunity to fulfill the cry of Moses for all of God's people to be prophets. We are to carry the Elijah anointing in preparing for the return of the Lord in the same way that John the Baptist carried the Elijah anointing and prepared the people for the coming of the Lord.

So how do we prepare for an increase of power in our lives?

By having our minds renewed to a Kingdom mind-set. This helps us to take the risks necessary for God's promised invasion.

By asking for more of the Holy Spirit. Divine encounters given to hungry people have always been the most important part of a person's transformation. Wise men still travel. Go wherever you need to go to receive what others can contribute to this need.

By giving honor to the gifts of Christ[19]—past and present. Recognizing the grace of God on leaders outside of your immediate "stream" is beneficial in becoming the whole person He has designed. I have made it a practice to even honor the descendents of revivalists, asking them for the prayer of blessing and impartation for me to fulfill my assignment.

Put yourself in places where you can encounter the presence of God and allow the power of the Holy Spirit to transform your thoughts until you find yourself dreaming with God of the possibilities and potential realities in bringing Heaven to earth. Out of that encounter a lifestyle develops that sustains revival in our own lives. Once in place, we help to create a culture that sustains revival. It looks somewhat like this:

A culture that sustains revival is a culture captivated by the Lord Jesus Christ, delighting in the presence of the Holy Spirit.

It is a culture of humility—recognizing that we can do nothing except what we see the Father doing and only that insofar as we receive the empowerment of the Holy Spirit.

This culture releases the power of God. To not walk in power is to withhold from man the very encounter that would bring God praise.

This culture releases the report of God's glory, nature, and covenant: keeping continuously on our lips the testimony of what God is doing...not just what He has done in the past.

It is a culture of honor that recognizes people's gifts and works hard to call out people's destiny. As destinies are released, we ensure that the revival continues growing from glory to glory in subsequent generations.

It seeks to defer to others rather than compete, bless rather than destroy through petty jealousies, and seeks not to criticize but to aspire to have the mind of Christ and the heart of compassion for those in our midst and outside the church walls.

It is a culture that extends the blessings of God outward rather than hoarding them for ourselves.

It is a culture where corporate gatherings open us up to greater encounters with the living God. Where the glory[20] brings unity and divine encounters release us to fulfill our destiny—to release Heaven on earth wherever we go.

This is the assignment of the hour. And I joyfully welcome an increased manifestation of the Holy Spirit that enabled Jesus to pursue and display an authentic Gospel. It is that same Spirit that raised Jesus from the dead that resides within us. But He's not in us as a lake. He's in us as a river that must be released.[21] It is that River that will change the landscape of the world around us.

Concluding Prayer

When Mary, the mother of Jesus, was confronted with the angel, she was astonished. When she heard the promise of her giving birth to the Messiah, she was even more shocked. Yet she prayed a prayer that has become a standard for all who are required to embrace a promise that goes beyond our comprehension: *"Let it be to me according to your word."* [22] In light of His promises for this day, that has, out of necessity, become my prayer.

ABOUT THE WRITER:

BILL JOHNSON pastors Bethel Church in Redding, California, and has a growing international reputation as a man who challenges the faith of all who hear him or read his books—in particular, *When Heaven Invades Earth* and *The Supernatural Power of the Transformed Mind*. The School of Supernatural Ministry, housed at Bethel Church, is one of the fastest growing and more provocative schools in the nation. Bill and his staff are forerunners in developing New Creation Power Brokers of the Holy Spirit, calling out their God-ordained destinies and sending them out into their particular spheres of influence. His focus on helping others develop a culture that sustains revival has been embraced by pastors around the world.

———

ENDNOTES

All Scripture references in this chapter are from the New King James Version.

1. John 5:19.

2. John 14:12.

3. 1 Corinthians 14:1.

4. Acts 1:4,5.

5. Acts 2:4.

6. Ephesians 5:18, *"be filled with the Spirit."*

7. Exalting knowledge above experience is one of the Western Church's greatest areas of deception.

8. Ephesians 1:3.

9. 1 Thessalonians 5:19.

10. Ephesians 4:30.

11. I define religion as "form without power."

12. Zechariah 12:8.

13. Matthew 13:33.

14. Haggai 2:7.

15. Hebrews 11:10.

16. 2 Corinthians 3:18.

17. Isaiah 9:7.

18. Matthew 25:25.

19. Ephesians 4:7-13.

20. John 17:22.

21. John 7:38,39.

22. Luke 1:38.

CHAPTER 11

Preparing for an Increase in Authority

BY MAHESH CHAVDA

God is calling you to a new level of authority, new level of anointing, new level of boldness, and a new level of confidence. Know that you serve a living God and He is the One who is giving you power and authority. We have seen this authority bring deliverance and healing to countless people in the course of our ministry. I believe that we are going to see a dramatic increase in supernatural power—going from Mach 1 to Mach 10, from breaking the sound barrier to ten times the speed of sound. Yet some of the victories we seek will not come until we learn to fast and pray—individually and corporately, as a church.

One of the most outstanding miracles I have seen was in Milwaukee, Wisconsin. A Hispanic gentleman, who had heard about our ministry and the miracles that happened, brought his 5-year-old child to the hotel ballroom where I was holding a miracle service. This child had epileptic seizures all his life. I was just surprised that the child had not been bedridden and unable to function because he had seizures about every 2 to 5 minutes. I sensed a demon peering out of the eyes of the child and knew that I was confronting a major demonic stronghold.

"Lord," I prayed silently, "I didn't have a chance to prepare for this confrontation."

Yet the Lord replied, "You've already prepared yourself by prayer and fasting."

Heartened by His reply, I confronted that thing and said, "In the name of Jesus, you have tormented this child long enough. His father, who has the authority over him, has brought him to the servants of Jesus, and I tell you this is the last day that you're going to be here. Your time is over. You go where Jesus sends you, but you will no longer stay in this child; in the name of Jesus, leave!"

Something snapped in the heavenlies. The smell of burning sulfur and rotting eggs filled the ballroom like the most horrible smell of rotting flesh you can imagine. Everyone smelled it. It filled the room then slowly filtered out. The boy was instantly made whole, totally delivered. I was so grateful watching the father's face, tears streaming down, holding his son with joy knowing that the boy's seizures had stopped just as in the scripture in Matthew 17:18: *Jesus rebuked, the demon, and it came out of the him, and the child was cured from that very hour.* (NKJV)

This was just one of thousands upon thousands of miracles I have seen God work through our ministry. I credit them to His loving presence and power, yet my years spent with Him during long seasons of prayer and fasting birthed within me an intimacy that enabled me to carry His authority into many situations and bring deliverance.

How does fasting really work? I don't know all the answers because this is one of God's great mysteries, but I can share what I have learned up to this point. For one thing, demons get very uncomfortable when Christians begin fasting. We know from the Scriptures that many of the diseases, ailments, mental problems, and chronic behavioral problems afflicting mankind are instigated or perpetuated by demonic forces who want to hinder God's people and generally torment God's highest creation.

Fasting shows a desperation and determination to "touch the Lord," who alone is the source of all healing. Demons cannot stay around too long when a person fasts, because fasting unto God creates a totally different atmosphere that welcomes the Holy and repels the unholy. That is why demonic spirits get very uncomfortable around a person who fasts.

Anyone who is in a healing and deliverance ministry of any kind should make fasting part of his or her regular lifestyle. It is the spiritual equivalent of an athlete working out at a gym. As you fast and seek God's face, He will begin to plant an authority in you born out of intimacy with Him that demons will recognize and fear. In addition, Isaiah 58 lists 12 specific benefits of the fast "the Lord has chosen:"

◆ Revelation

◆ Healing and wholeness

◆ Righteousness

◆ The presence of the *shekinah* glory of God

◆ Answered prayers

◆ Continual guidance

◆ Contentment

◆ Refreshing

◆ Strength

◆ Work that endures

◆ Raising up of future generations

◆ Restoration

He has called us to fast and pray, and then to obey. At that point, He can release apostolic anointing into our lives, our churches, and our ministry in the world. With this anointing, our ministry will not be apologetic, half-hearted, or apathetic. It will not be laced with fear, doubt, or unbelief. It will be prophetic and apostolic, fitted with a double-edged sharpness that comes only through the Holy Spirit. We will be gently confrontational without even thinking about it, much as the Lord led me to pray a simple prayer of command through which God literally destroyed the seat of satan in a town in Zaire.

I was conducting a mass evangelism campaign in the city of Kananga, Zaire, an area gripped by sorcery. This crusade conducted by our ministry was the first ever held in that area by those filled with the power of the Holy Spirit and things were going well. This was despite the aggressive opposition of powerful witch doctors who had dominated the area for many years. Right from the start they came to publicly pronounce curses on us. Most of the people feared these servants of satan. I was told by the people there, "These witch doctors have the power to tell someone, 'You will die in seven days,' and the person will drop dead on the seventh day."

Our meetings made these witch doctors so angry that they called in every witch doctor in the whole region for a meeting to figure out how to stop us from proclaiming Christ. These witch doctors gathered together beneath the branches of a towering tree used by sorcerers for many generations. They believed that spiritual power for evil emanated from this "sorcerer's tree" and it was here that the witch doctors conducted evil ceremonies and ate human flesh as they cast spells on our crusade being held some miles away.

On the final night of the crusade, the sorcerers again gathered beneath the "magic" sorcerer's tree to conduct demonic worship and rituals, cursing Christians, eating human flesh, and discussing plans on how to stop the crusade (since nothing they had already tried was working).

At the end of my message that night, the Lord told me to break the yoke of witchcraft over that region and loose the people from its power. While the sorcerers raged beneath their tree, I declared before thousands of people gathered there, "Satan, I bind you. I take authority over the spirit of witchcraft, and I break the curse of sorcery over this area!"

In that moment, according to the reports of several eye-witnesses from the area where the witch doctors were gathered, flames of fire streaked across the sky, spanning the approximately 7-to-8 mile distance from the crusade to fall upon the sorcerer's tree. The fire instantly set the tree ablaze. The branches, which were spread 34 feet across, were consumed from the top down! It did not split the trunk or branches as would normally happen to a tree struck by lightning. The tree trunk burned for three days until it was consumed down to the height of a man's head. It still stands today like a burnt matchstick, a mute reminder of the power of the name of Jesus!

We learned the details of this miracle from some of the witch doctors themselves. They said that when the fire came down and ignited the tree some of the witch doctors were blinded, some were burned, and some of them repented when they saw the overwhelming power of God. They came to us with the story and asked us how to be saved.

When I visited the site of the tree and stood before the charred trunk marking all that remained of satan's evil grip on that area, I was reminded of Elijah's confrontation with the prophets of Baal in First Kings 18. My spirit leapt within me, and I cried out as did Elisha of old when the mantle of anointing fell on him, *"Where is the Lord God of Elijah?"* (2 Kings 2:14 NKJV).

Elisha was thirsty. He was hungry to see the manifested power of the living God pass to his generation as Elijah was taken into Heaven. He confronted the demonic powers of his day and the people stood on Mount Carmel watching in awe. Centuries later, Jesus confronted the powers of His generation once and forever. And the people stood on the mountains listening to Him in awe. Even today, the Church stands, as it were, gazing into Heaven, expecting Jesus to do from Heaven what He has empowered us to do through the Holy Spirit on earth. The magnitude of God's move in our generation demands that we step down from the mount of spiritual paralysis, take up the mantle of anointing and power Jesus gave us, and begin to obey His commands.

He has called us to fast and pray, and then to obey. He wants us to learn the lessons of prayer and fasting so well that He can send us out to our generation *in the power of the Spirit.* If prayer is the booster capsule containing our gifts and requests to God, then fasting is the booster rocket that propels us from Mach 1 to Mach 10, which lifts our prayers beyond the boundaries of earth and into the heavenlies.

I see the Church poised in virtually the same place the prophet Elijah was when he prayed for rain on Mount Carmel after he had prophesied to the evil King Ahab that rain was coming to end a three-year drought. At first there wasn't a cloud in the sky, but he kept praying. After a long drought in the Church, we have prophesied that that the rains are coming, and like Elijah, we are perched on a high place with our faces between our knees. And the

Church is beginning to hear the sound of the abundance of rain! We have seen the first raindrops of God's glory descend in such places as Argentina; Brazil; Toronto, Ontario; and Pensacola, Florida. It is like Elijah's cloud, small as a man's hand, starting to rise out of the sea. But it is not enough. The abundance of rain is coming.

By praying and fasting together, we can overcome every hindrance, obstruction, and mountain that blocks the way between us and our corporate destiny and calling in Christ! Victory is only found in the realm of the Spirit, and that is why the devil takes every opportunity to divert us from the mode of prayer and fasting back into the natural mode...a mode of spiritual paralysis as we watch others move in the anointing. Many leaders have called the Church to pray and fast in the past. But it is a calling that is now and forever...while the bridegroom is away. Fasting reveals to Heaven the love-hunger that resides in our hearts for the Lord. And it is this love-hunger that moves Heaven to respond.

I believe that God wants the Church to get into the mode of fasting and praying now because He knows that it will be necessary if we are going to come into the fullness of our apostolic anointing for miracles, signs, and wonders. The Lord is asking us today, "Will you be a people who will see the vision—My vision—and be willing to pay the price through prayer and fasting?"

Now let me bring it closer to home: Local revival and global harvest will never happen unless we become personally involved in the purposes of God through prayer and fasting—not just as individuals, but as corporate entities.

At All Nations Church, the church Bonnie and I have pastored for more than a decade, we have incorporated set times of prayer through our Friday night Watch of the Lord and annual corporate fasts of 21 and 40 days as a church body. The results are amazing to watch as people become personally involved and committed to God's vision for individuals to be completely set free from demonic spirits and healed of life-challenging and life-threatening illnesses.

In recent years, during our corporate fasts for individuals who specifically attend our church, we have seen medically-documented healings of a teenager who was healed of severe Tourette's Syndrome, which included healing of many obsessive-compulsive disorder traits, and another boy healed of severe autism, which included healing many of his physical problems, among other miracles. What the world sees as incurable is entirely in the realm of possibility for a praying and fasting church. Nothing is impossible with God.

The community is being trained to love and welcome the anointing and honor the King of Glory. I feel like God is moving us toward another level of anointing which is more corporate. That is where the commanded blessing of the Lord comes upon us and we learn to dwell together in unity. As a church given to prayer and fasting, we are seeing a shift in the apostolic anointing that heralds the sound of the coming of rain—the glory of God fills our house in tangible ways.

During one conference held in our church building (a tent at that time), a glory cloud appeared.

I was preaching to nearly 1,000 people gathered in the tent when I shifted into singing Second Corinthians 3, "Where the Spirit of the Lord is, there is liberty." Suddenly the cloud of His presence manifested in the middle of the tent. Hundreds of people started shouting out about the glory cloud. Others stood in total awe. At first I didn't realize what was happening until people started pointing. The cloud floated above us, beaming with light and glittery gold-like particles. It stayed almost half an hour.

It was quite inspiring and way beyond anything we had actually seen. Other pastors said it was the first time they had seen a manifestation of the presence. The moment released a great sense of love and honor for the Lord Jesus in our midst. We were so humbled. That was one of the marks of the next level that I believe we are going toward.

The Lord said He would take us from glory to glory as individuals. But His grace is more fully revealed to us as we recognize ourselves as parts of the corporate body. I believe that this release of God's glory to the Church results in a corporate anointing that will reside in many churches. In the months and years to come, the world will recognize that there are places where God is manifest and that those places are where miracles happen. Will you be a part of that? Will you and your church pay the price of prayer and fasting for breakthrough?

The key to defeating dark strongholds that imprison children and adults in medical and emotional despair, the key to taking authority over powers of the occult, calming the winds and the sea, walking on water, and releasing divine healing and restoration, is twofold.

First we must tap the power of the Spirit through the combination of prayer and fasting; and second, we will overcome the largest battles in this generation only when we pray and fast together and unleash the incredible power of the Body of Christ on its knees. Doing the works of Jesus begins with prayer and fasting (as He did throughout His ministry on earth) because these were the first works of Jesus in His mission to destroy the works of the enemy.

ABOUT THE WRITER:

MAHESH CHAVDA is the founder and senior pastor of All Nations Church in Charlotte, North Carolina. An international evangelist, Mahesh and his wife, Bonnie, have led more than 700,000 people to the Lord worldwide. They are New Creation Power Brokers of the Holy Spirit with a ministry characterized by signs and wonders, miracles, healing, and deliverance. The ministry school housed at All Nations Church, focuses on mentoring others to become ones who make God radiant to all they meet and take the power of God into their spheres of influence—whether at home, at work, in the mission field, or in their churches. They are prolific authors of such classics as, *The Hidden Power of Prayer and Fasting* and *The Hidden Power of the Blood of Christ.*

Bibliography

Addison, Doug. *Prophesy, Dreams & Evangelism*. N. Sutton, New Hampshire: Streams Publishing House, 2005.

Chavda, Mahesh. *The Hidden Power of the Blood of Jesus*. Shippensburg, PA: Destiny Image Publishers, 2004.

Chavda, Mahesh. *Only Love Can Make a Miracle*. Shippensburg, PA: Destiny Image Publishers, 2002.

Clark, Randy. *Lighting Fires*. Lake Mary, FL: Charisma House, 1998.

Clark, Randy. *There is More!* Harrisburg, PA: Global Awakening, 2006.

Cooke, Graham. *A Divine Confrontation: Birth Pangs of the New Church*. Shippensburg, PA: Destiny Image Publishers, 1999.

Cooke, Graham. *Approaching the Heart of Prophecy, A Journey into Encouragement, Blessing and Prophetic Gifting*. Winston-Salem, NC: Punch Press, 2006.

Davis, Paul Keith. *Engaging the Revelatory Realms of Heaven*. N. Sutton, New Hampshire: Streams Publishing House, 2003.

Foster, Richard J. *The Challenge of the Disciplined Life*. New York: HarperCollins Publishers, 1985.

Goll, Jim and Michal Ann. *Encounters with a Supernatural God*. Shippensburg, PA: Destiny Image Publishers, Inc., 1998.

Hamon, Bill. *Apostles, Prophets, and the Coming Moves of God*. Shippensburg, PA: Destiny Image Publishers, Inc., 1997.

Hamon, Bill. *The Day of the Saints*. Shippensburg, PA: Destiny Image Publishers, Inc., 2002.

Hauser, Tom. *Breaking Free from Darkness—A Practical Guide to Deliverance*. Wilmington, NC: Vineyard Community Church, 2005.

Hornberger, Francine. *The World's Greatest Psychics*. New York: Citadel Press, 2004.

Jackson, Bill. *The Quest for the Radical Middle—A History of the Vineyard*. Cape Town, South Africa: Vineyard International Publishing, 1999.

Johnson, Bill. *When Heaven Invades Earth*. Shippensburg, PA: Destiny Image Publishers, Inc., 2003.

Joyner, Rick. *The Prophetic Ministry*. Charlotte, NC: MorningStar Publications, 1997.

King, Patricia. *Spiritual Revolution*. Shippensburg, PA: Destiny Image Publishers, Inc., 2006.

Koch, Dr. Kurt E. *Christian Counseling and Occultism*. Grand Rapids, MI: Kregal Publications, 1972.

McIntyre, Joe. *E.W. Kenyon and his Message of Faith*. Lake Mary, FL: Charisma House, 1997.

Nee, Watchman. *The Latent Power of the Soul*. New York: Christian Fellowship Publications, 1972.

Otis, George. *The Twilight Labyrinth*. Grand Rapids, MI: Chosen Books, 1997.

Peck, M. Scott. *Glimpses of the Devil: A Psychiatrist's Personal Accounts of Possession, Exorcism and Redemption*. New York: Free Press/Simon & Schuster, Inc., 2005.

Pierce, Cal. *Preparing the Way: The Reopening of the John G. Lake Healing Rooms*. Hagerstown, MD: McDougal Publishing, 2001.

Sandford, John. *Elijah Among Us*. Grand Rapids, MI: Chosen Books, 2002.

Sandford, John. *The Elijah Task*. Tulsa, OK: Victory House, 1977.

Stott, John R.W. *The Baptism and Fullness of the Holy Spirit.* London: Inter-Varsity Fellowship, 1964.

Torrey, R.A. *The Best of R.A. Torrey.* Grand Rapids, MI: Baker, 1990.

Vallotton, Kris and Bill Johnson. *The Supernatural Ways of Royalty.* Shippensburg, PA: Destiny Image Publishers, Inc., 2006.

About the Author

JULIA LOREN earned degrees in both journalism (B.A., University of Washington) and counseling psychology (M.S., Seattle Pacific University) which, according to her, means that she is a doubly-trained skeptic. Through the years, however, the manifest presence of God and His love opened her heart and mind to receive a much higher education in things pertaining to the Holy Spirit.

She is the author of *The Note on the Mirror* (Zondervan, 1990), *Engle v. Vitale: The End of School Prayer* (Greenhaven, 2000), *Healing the Wounds of Open Adoption* (Adoption Counsel Press, 2000), *Healing the Wounds of Closed Adoption* (Adoption Counsel Press, 2000), and the Glimpses of Jesus series – *Breaking the Spirit of Despair* and *Dancing in the Fullness of Joy* (Tharseo Publishing, 2006). She is also a frequent contributor to *Charisma* magazine and other Christian publications.

Shifting Shadows of Supernatural Power and its sequel, *Shifting Shadows of Spiritual Experiences*, focus on increasing awareness of this current move of God, bringing both discernment and balance to readers, and motivating all believers to take their place in the plan unfolding during this generation of time.

Author Contact Information

You can learn more about Julia Loren and her books by viewing her Website:

www.julialoren.net.

Interested in having Julia come to your church or conference?
Please contact her at:

juliascribes@yahoo.com.

Coming Soon

Shifting Shadows of Spiritual Experiences

by James Goll and Julia Loren

(Destiny Image Publishers, Inc.)

This second book in the Shifting Shadows series examines the most common spiritual experiences reported by individuals around the world—visions, angel sightings, out-of-body-experiences, teleportation, near death experiences, encounters with "ghosts," and other supernatural encounters. How can you tell if a spiritual experience is from God, satan, or one that originates in your own soul? This book will launch you into a greater measure of discernment and catapult your faith into new encounters with the spiritual realms of God.

Glimpses of Jesus Series
by Julia Loren

Breaking the Spirit of Despair
Dancing in the Fullness of Joy
Receiving the Crown of Courage

This series of short, interactive journals include testimonies of healing, powerful scriptures, and visions of Christ's healing presence. The greatest demonic onslaught against the Church is the spirit of despair – paralyzing many with depression and anxiety. The first book will unlock doors to healing anxiety and depression. The second book will release the fullness of joy to your life. The third book will refresh the weary, reinstate ministries, and grant courage to fulfill destinies. Get ready to dance in the fullness of joy and run the race with courage.

Available at Christian bookstores and at www.julialoren.net

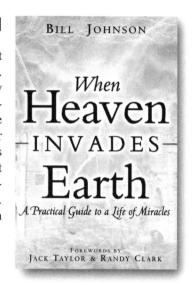
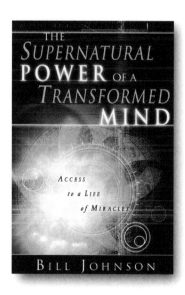

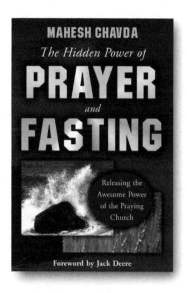

THE HIDDEN POWER OF THE BLOOD OF JESUS

In this pop Christian culture many believers have never been exposed to the great truths upon which the Church of Jesus Christ has been built. One of those forgotten truths is the purpose and power of the blood of Jesus. We sing about it in our hymns, there is power in the blood, but few of us have experienced the realty of those words.

ISBN 0-7684-2222-1

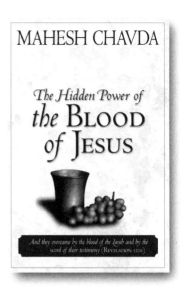

THE HIDDEN POWER OF HEALING PRAYER

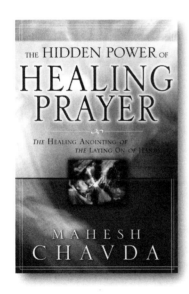

Here is the fatal blow to the belief that God does not heal today. Through the power of his personal experience and strength of his biblical insight, Mahesh Chavda reveals how the healing compassion of our Lord reaches the hurting masses simply by the believer's healing touch. Written with compassion, humor, and insight, The Hidden Power of Healing Prayer affirms that the healing anointing and the gifts of signs and wonders are not reserved for *super saints* or the specially gifted, but are available to every believer who carries the compassion and love of the Lord Jesus.

ISBN 0-7684-2303-1

Additional copies of this book and other
book titles from DESTINY IMAGE are
available at your local bookstore.

Call toll-free: 1-800-722-6774.

Send a request for a catalog to:

Destiny Image® Publishers, Inc.
P.O. Box 310
Shippensburg, PA 17257-0310

*"Speaking to the Purposes of God for this
Generation and for the Generations to Come."*

For a complete list of our titles,
visit us at www.destinyimage.com